LIVES
in the
BALANCE

LIVES *in the* BALANCE

Improving Accountability for Public Spending in Developing Countries

CHARLES C. GRIFFIN, DAVID DE FERRANTI,
COURTNEY TOLMIE, JUSTIN JACINTO,
GRAEME RAMSHAW, AND CHINYERE BUN

RESULTS FOR DEVELOPMENT INSTITUTE

BROOKINGS INSTITUTION PRESS

WASHINGTON, DC

Copyright © 2010
Results for Development Institute
1875 Connecticut Avenue NW, Suite 1210
Washington, DC 20009
www.resultsfordevelopment.org

and

The Brookings Institution
1775 Massachusetts Avenue NW
Washington, DC 20036
www.brookings.edu

Lives in the Balance: Improving Accountability for Public Spending in Developing Countries may be ordered from:
BROOKINGS INSTITUTION PRESS
c/o HFS, P.O. Box 50370, Baltimore, MD 21211-4370
Tel.: 1-800-537-5487 or 410-516-6956; Fax: 410-516-6998; www.brookings.edu

Library of Congress Cataloging-in-Publication data
Lives in the balance : improving accountability for public spending in developing countries / Charles Griffin ... [et al.].
    p.   cm.
Includes bibliographical references and index.
ISBN 978-0-8157-3289-1 (pbk. : alk. paper)
  1. Developing countries—Appropriations and expenditures—Evaluation. 2. Government spending policy--Developing countries. 3. Government accountability—Developing countries. I. Griffin, Charles C., 1951– II. Title.
  HJ7980.L58 2010
  352.4'6091724—dc22   2010021129

Editing and typesetting by Communications Development Incorporated, Washington, DC

Cover design by Terry Patton Rhodes

Contents

Boxes

Figures

Tables

Preface—a story about this book

An experienced World Bank economist takes on the assignment of preparing a public expenditure review for a country in Sub-Saharan Africa. The previous one, prepared three years earlier, focused on infrastructure and maintenance. The economist, based in Washington, develops a work plan with an economist based in the local World Bank office. Between them, they spend 40 weeks on the task. This will be the first public expenditure review in 10 years to focus on the social sectors, so they draw on 4 weeks of time each from a Washington-based education economist and a health specialist who work on the country and know the sectors well. They use a smattering of time from two other local consultants, who visit several districts to gather information on how funds are distributed to schools and medical facilities.

The work begins in September. The entire group visits the capital city for two weeks to gather information on this year's budget, review allocations and actual expenditures during the previous three years, and talk to officials. They spend an enormous amount of time pulling the budget data together and trying to interpret it in discussions with staff in the ministry of finance. They find household survey data to connect beneficiaries to the spending patterns. They visit every donor to get estimates of how much is spent and on what, since most donor financing does not enter the government's budget. They return in February with their initial analysis complete, to pursue questions they have with government staff and donors. By April they have completed a first draft of the report.

The report is reviewed in Washington during a two-hour meeting by video conference chaired by the locally based country director. The meeting discusses the analysis and conclusions of the report, which show little change from the previous social sector review 10 years ago—relatively low spending on education and health, with a large share going to subsidize universities and hospitals. Because higher income citizens have better access to these services, they continue to capture a disproportionate share of benefits. Donors finance books for primary schools and medicines for health clinics; otherwise, the situation would be even worse. Districts continue to serve as pass-through mechanisms, with little power to tailor spending decisions to local conditions and no accountability. The district officials who were visited complain that books arrive at the schools six months after the term starts and that health clinics face "stockouts" of basic drugs and supplies virtually every week. Infrastructure is dilapidated. Teachers and medical personnel complain that the government is three months behind in paying their salaries, which consume more than 90 percent of the budget in education and 85 percent in health.

How could this situation persist with almost no change over 10 years? Why are conditions so similar in other countries? How can the World Bank country director and the authors convince the government to change these patterns so that systems deliver and poor people get the investments they need in schooling and health to improve their lives? How can donors be convinced to coordinate better among themselves and with the government to boost the impact of their spending?

The World Bank's portfolio includes five-year projects in education and health that have disbursed only about 10 percent of their committed funds despite having been under way for three years. The education project includes funding for books on the condition that the ministry of education shift to competitive procurement. The ministry argues that there are not enough local book publishers and that the World Bank, by withholding the funds, is depriving children of books. The bank stands firm, so the money remains unspent. Money for school rehabilitation is also stuck because the ministry of public works, which must undertake the construction or contract for it, is overwhelmed with higher priority road projects. A year ago the bank agreed to reallocate some of these funds to an already begun refurbishment of the ministry of education building so that at least some funds were being disbursed and to improve its relationship with the ministry in hopes of getting needed policy changes. A third chunk of money would go directly to schools for the headmaster to allocate, but systems are not yet in place to allow that to happen.

The result? Almost no disbursement from this loan except for the ministry building. Recently, disbursements in the health project were suspended because of a corruption investigation into bid rigging for pharmaceuticals. The country director wonders how the institution got into the position of knowing what needs to be done for more than a decade but being unable to influence the result, even with its own lending.

Subsequently, the prime minister convenes the cabinet to discuss these findings. Some around the table question the underlying data, the interpretation, and the World Bank's priorities. The minister of finance points out that spending on education and health has been rising, just not as fast as the bank staff think it should. With rapid population growth, he argues, it is impossible to hope for large increases in spending per student. The health system is just barely able to expand the immunization program each year to keep up with need—even that would be impossible without donor assistance. The minister of education suggests that the spending on universities is a result of success in getting more children through secondary school. He further argues that the World Bank wants to limit the country to primary education so that it cannot compete with countries in the West and that it is trying to destroy local book publishers by letting foreigners print books for the schools. The minister of health wonders how to reduce spending on hospitals when they are overflowing with patients. The rural clinics are hardly used—why put more money into them? More hospitals are needed, not fewer. "We are paying huge amounts of money to send patients to London for hospital care. We need to invest in our national hospital to save that money."

The result is a polite appreciation for the World Bank's work but the conclusion that little can be done to improve the situation without a large expansion of the budget, given the competing priorities that the government must deal with. The International Monetary Fund and the World Bank, the finance minister argues, will not accept such an expansion of overall spending. So, six months later the government approves the public expenditure review, and it is published. It goes on the World Bank's website. No local newspapers write about it. Almost no one in the country, other than the government staff directly involved, knows of its existence. It is never translated into any local languages.

Meanwhile, civil society organizations in several communities start to agitate because the children in their primary schools have to share books. And those books showed up only after school had been in session for three months, replacing books that had been in use for four years and had fallen apart. The new books are so valuable that the headmaster locks them in a cabinet at the end of each day, so children cannot take them home to study.

The books are just the tip of the iceberg. Students sit on dirt floors because the desks disappeared long ago. There is no money to repair school roofs, so the dirt floors turn into mud when it rains. Civil society organizations visit the district education officer to voice their complaints. They are told no money is anticipated for the rest of the year to make repairs or buy desks. And while more books are expected as publishers in the capital city get them printed, the publishers claim to be experiencing a paper shortage. Appalled, the civil society organizations take their case to the capital and gain an audience with the minister of education. He tells them that the ministry is doing the best that it can, but it simply has no resources to solve the problems.

The civil society organizations bring along several women who run small businesses to visit the ministry of finance to find out why teachers do not receive their salaries on time. After hours of waiting, they finally get an audience with a young man at the social sector desk who is sympathetic and too inexperienced to know how to obfuscate. "Yes, we know it is a problem. We have to move cash around to pay the bills. We have to make sure the civil servants in the capital get paid or we would have trouble here. We have to make sure the army gets paid on time. I hate to admit it, but the least likely to cause us trouble are teachers and health workers scattered in small towns." The women leave not believing a word of this explanation, however plausible it sounded. How could the government get itself stretched so thin that it can't pay its bills? What kind of prioritization puts paying teachers last? Does paying slowly just put the central bureaucrats in a position to ask for bribes from rural residents, who have no alternative but to pay? What is going on?

With further investigation, the civil society organizations discover that one book publisher has been awarded a monopoly to print all books for grades 1–5. It did get them printed, but three months later than the contract stipulated. The books are now sitting in ministry of education warehouses around the country, while the ministry itself slowly delivers them to schools. The publishers have no responsibility for getting the books to schools.

The civil society organizations also discover that the central ministry building is being refurbished and that a new administration building is being constructed at the national university. They cannot find out from anyone what these projects cost, but after searching the newspapers for coverage of the groundbreaking ceremonies, they read speeches boasting that the ministry of education project will cost $10 million over three years, financed by the World Bank, and that the new university building will take three years and cost $22 million, financed by a bilateral donor. Their back-of-the envelope calculations suggest that the $11 million being spent on those projects this year could finance repairs in 7,000 classrooms if communities pitched in to provide some of the labor. Just scaling back the plans would release funds to help with the classrooms.

The civil society organizations are indignant. Their children depend on a government that chooses not to pay its teachers on time and that lacks the sense to procure textbooks competitively or to require the publishers to arrange on-time delivery. Why can't head teachers just go out and buy the books directly in the market? The government invests in shiny new buildings for itself in the capital while primary schools are crumbling. The World Bank is a willing partner in this mess. Is it corruption or incompetence? Is it bad intentions? Is it an international plot to keep them poor?

They visit the legislator for their district. "I cannot do much about this problem," he says. "Have you ever seen the government's budget? It is impossible to understand what the money goes for and why it is spent the way it is. We get a jumble of numbers here a couple of weeks before we are supposed to pass the budget but with almost no ability to interpret it or to understand the priorities. There is no time for the ministries to discuss the budget with us. When the prime minister comes to give the budget speech, we hear the big picture and we pass the budget, but we almost never get into the details.

"The most I can do is to get a little money for new classrooms each year, because that is in the development budget, where we have some input. If it is in the regular budget—and that is where maintenance, salaries, books, and so on sit—it is almost completely controlled by the ministry of education. Our only tool is to vote down the whole budget proposal, but that would stop the entire government from functioning. Besides, I am in the same party as the government, so I have to vote for the budget.

"You are complaining about spending on the ministry's headquarters building and the university. If you look outside of education, the priorities only get worse. Do you realize that $100 million a year is spent to subsidize petrol for people like me to drive our cars? How many parents in your town even own a car? And that amount is a drop in the bucket relative to how much the state banks cost the government because of their bad lending practices. Could any of you even imagine qualifying for a loan from a state bank? We finance seriously ill people to go to London for hospital care. How many people in your town could even get to the capital if they needed care at the national hospital? Don't get me started. There is no excuse for our education system to fail our people. It is all a matter of priorities and making government work for all of us. There is corruption everywhere, but even if everyone were perfectly honest, the results would not be much better. The lack of accountability means it's easy to be corrupt, but it's also easy to make bad decisions that get us nowhere."

Taken aback, the civil society organizations decide that if even their member of parliament has given up, it was time for them to do something! While they might not be able to solve the book problem or the teacher pay problem, they could mount a campaign to do something about the classroom problem. They take to the streets in the capital. They document the state of their schools. They contrast dilapidated classrooms with the shining temples for education bureaucrats in the capital. Newspapers take up the cause. Other organizations around the country recognize the same problems in their towns. It becomes a national movement. The World Bank is vilified, and the minister of education eventually resigns. With pleasure and embarrassment the World Bank responds to the ministry of finance's request to reallocate textbook funding for school construction and to scale back the financing for the headquarters building. The ministry of finance changes its rules. Now headmasters organize classroom rehabilitation following approval by the school board. They shop locally and post the construction schedule and costs for all to see at the school. Ministry of finance personnel in each district take responsibility for paying the bills.

Suddenly things are moving. The World Bank takes the opportunity to pressure the ministry of education to use the same mechanism to move funds from the loan so that headmasters will have cash for incidentals, following an annual plan monitored by the school board and posted for all to see. Despite ministry of education resistance, based on the belief that schools are incapable of handling funds, pressure from the ministry of finance helps to make it happen. Other donors, encouraged by the direct conduit to schools and accountability at the school itself, volunteer to put more of their funds through the same channel.

The civil society organizations are jubilant. They had a tangible impact. What cause could they take up now? Could they hope to fix the textbook problem? Could they get teachers paid on time while also finding a way to require better performance? Could they leverage their new-found power to get permanent increases in funding for primary schools? Could they argue for supplemental funding for poorer areas? What about opportunities for children in rural areas to get into secondary school? Could they get the World Bank thrown out of the country?

A visionary leader among the civil society organizations begins to understand that to make a lasting impact, they would have to move beyond the issue orientation that has proved so successful and develop the capability to get deeply into policy issues in education and into the nuts and bolts of education budgets and how to influence long-term changes in priorities. They would have to learn how the system works if they wanted to influence it. That would mean acquiring formal analytic capability without losing the engagement and advocacy capability that they had developed over the past three years.

The minister of finance is not happy with how this situation has played out. He is lucky to keep his job while shifting the blame to the minister of education.

But he knows that he has been equally to blame for not being more inventive in addressing problems in education that he and everyone else had been well aware of for years. He has to admit that he likes the result—a better system of oversight for school funding, and for not much more money, they have begun to chip away at the problems in education that had emerged from decades of putting funds into a broken system. He begins to wonder how to address some of the other problems, like teacher performance and textbook procurement, without spending too much money. The ministry of education has always complained that the problem is woefully inadequate funding. Maybe that is wrong. And in any event, this new experience suggests that a better system of priority setting and accountability might attract more outside funding.

The country director at the World Bank and his staff laugh ruefully. "How did we get into this situation? We knew what was wrong, and we tried to use our funding to fix it. We couldn't get the ministry of education to budge, and the rest of the government felt powerless to do anything because the price tag seemed too high. It took those little organizations that came out of nowhere to embarrass the government into doing something. We have been trying for 10 years to get funding to the schools; they were able to get it done in a matter of months. We've seen schools rehabbed across the country in three years—after years when the ministry of public works was hardly doing one school at a time with our loan funds. Just mock me if I ever let myself be convinced to paint another ministry of education headquarters."

This story is true—up to a point—and reflects the experience of one of the authors in the 1990s. It could as easily have been a montage of experiences in countries across continents because the routine is amazingly consistent. The story becomes a fantasy with this sentence: "Meanwhile, civil society organizations in several communities start to agitate because the children in their primary schools have to share books." The rest of the story is a vision about what could have happened had domestic organizations been able to monitor the government and demand change. The changes we dream of did not happen, and this country is still caught in a creeping and irregular cycle of donor-pushed reform 17 years later. This book is one small contribution to turn fantasy into reality.

Acknowledgments

Transformational moments are always much easier to see in hindsight than in foresight. But we believe that we are in a transformational moment. This book has had more than a three-year gestation as we tried to understand what feels like a sea change in the potential for public accountability around the world. So many factors are now lining up. Many more countries enjoy at least partial democratic openness. The technology of information is undergoing a revolution not seen since the invention of movable type. Communication costs have been plummeting everywhere for the past decade. Openness in public budgets and freedom of information laws are gaining traction. Well educated young people have been arriving on the scene in large numbers the world over. And new sources of funds have become available internationally to support civil society organizations. In the meantime, large international organizations and bilateral donors have discovered governance and are making it an integral part of their development agendas. We hope we have succeeded in making a little bit of sense of these changes, but we had a lot of help doing so.

This is one of three books that emerged from that effort. The other two are *How to Improve Governance: A Framework for Analysis and Action* (de Ferranti and others 2009), which develops and applies a framework for accountability that explicitly includes such civil society organizations as independent monitoring organizations, and *From the Ground Up: Improving Government Performance with Independent Monitoring Organizations* (Kosack, Tolmie, and Griffin 2010), which documents the work under a pilot competitive small grants program to support independent monitoring organizations in developing skills to monitor government spending and service delivery.

Throughout this process, we have received comments on drafts of this book and good advice from many probing minds. While the shortcomings of what we have produced are ours alone, we would like to recognize peer reviewers and advisers who have helped us, including Myrna Alexander, Kevin Bohrer, Anil Deolalikar, Linda Frey, Tom Heller, C.R. Hibbs, Warren Krafchik, and Smita Singh. Anil Deolalikar and Warren Krafchik have been critical partners for us, with equal weight on both words—we could not have done it without them, and they were generous with their constructive criticism.

Background papers commissioned for this study have been incorporated into this book. They are cited in the text and appear in the references. Thanks to Matt Andrews, Loren Becker, Anil Deolalikar, Amanda Glassman, Monica Jain, Jean-Jacques Lecat, Ngozi Okonjo-Iwela, Philip Osafo-Kwaako, Alfonso Sanchez, Jamil Sopher, Ray Struyk, and Vinod Vyasulu for their contributions as authors or coauthors. We are indebted also to many practitioners and academics, including our colleagues at the Brookings Institution, Results for Development, and the World Bank—a list far too long to include here—who gave seminars or sat on panels at Brookings as part of the development of the book. Others submitted to interviews as we tried to understand the landscape.

Omowunmi Ladipo of the World Bank coordinated the review of public financial management and procurement assessments in Latin America and the Caribbean. Without her enthusiastic collaboration, we would not have been able to connect these financial "plumbing and wiring manuals" to governance. Her colleagues Trichur K. Balakrishnan, V.S. Krishnakumar, and Irina Luca organized a similar effort in Sub-Saharan Africa that benefited from comments by other procurement and financial management staff in the region.

Bruce Ross-Larson was our coach extraordinaire on messages, content, and organization. He and his colleagues at Communications Development Incorporated, especially Meta de Coquereaumont, Christopher Trott, and Elaine Wilson, were exceptionally patient with us, conscientious, and creative in their editing and layout of the book. Tony Ody also helped us with his knowledgeable and speedy reading of a late version of the book, suggesting organizational improvements and even taking pen in hand to help edit.

Alice Krupit, Kyle Peppin, and Gina Reynosa assisted the project at Brookings. They managed seminars, grantees, and travel. And they managed the manuscript itself as it grew, changed, and eventually shrank. Courtney Heck now performs that job at Results for Development.

Carmen Hamaan and Anna Sant'anna helped us in the early stages to conceptualize the problem and to begin investigating organizations identifiable as independent monitoring organizations. They, along with Anil Deolalikar, Robert Hindle, Olivier Lafourcade, and Nick Warren, made early forays to visit organizations in Africa, Asia, and Latin America to understand their capabilities.

We are indebted to Lael Brainard, former Vice President of the Global Economy and Development Program at Brookings, and her team for their support. The financial support of the William and Flora Hewlett Foundation is gratefully acknowledged.

The process of government accountability—an anecdote and an agenda

In a study of the effectiveness of education spending programs, the National Center for Economic Research (CIEN) in Guatemala looked at why increased school spending was not being converted into improved education results. Only half of school-age Guatemalan children complete primary school, and reading and math skills are at dismally low levels. Several problems immediately became clear as researchers surveyed parents and primary school students and teachers. Some 62 percent of head teachers reported that textbooks had not arrived in time for the start of the 2008 school year, disrupting student learning. And 73 percent of school boards surveyed reported that the school meals program did not provide enough food for students who needed it.

Rather than simply write a report, CIEN researchers decided to use their results to promote changes that would make school spending more effective. Armed with policy recommendations based on their interviews and findings, the team worked with leaders from the Ministry of Education, convincing them to shift the start of the school year from January to February so that it no longer coincided with the start of the fiscal year, a major cause of the delays in the delivery of resources. CIEN also worked with students, teachers, and parents to encourage them to monitor government performance using CIEN's findings as a baseline. While the full impact of the policy shift and community monitoring efforts will not become clear for several more years, the changes encouraged by CIEN are important steps toward improving the effectiveness of school spending—and ultimately education achievement—in Guatemala.

*   *   *

This book addresses the challenge of achieving efficient and equitable use of public resources in developing countries in such sectors as education and health. The way stakeholders in the international arena think about economic and social development has changed considerably in recent years. Multilateral organizations and donors now have an array of tools for evaluating problems and introducing potential solutions in public expenditures. Improved transparency and understanding of public spending have accompanied the global trend toward democratization, which has also created space for traditionally voiceless groups—poor people, excluded ethnic and religious groups, women, and others—to become more involved in development. Civil society organizations have sprung up nearly everywhere to watch government and press for change.

Chapter 2 examines what we know about government expenditures and budget execution in a broad sample of low- and middle-income countries. Donors and multilateral organizations have encouraged governments to make their public spending programs more effective. Sometimes this support has yielded improvements. All too often the results have proved disappointing.

In asking why such efforts have frequently had limited impact, and what can be done to improve results, this book takes the view that the fundamental challenge is less technocratic than political: holding political officials and public employees accountable to the wider public (who pay the taxes and use the services) for the use they make of the public resources entrusted to them.

To explore the relationship between those who run the government and the people, the book uses the "principal-agent" model, as developed in chapter 3. In its original application the model was developed to analyze the conflicts of interest that can arise when the owner of a private firm engages a professional manager to run the firm. How can the owner feel confident that the manager is making decisions for the owner's benefit rather than the manager's? How can the owner monitor the manager's actions and develop incentives that align the manager's incentives with the owner's?

When considering government accountability, it can be helpful to think of politicians and public officials as the "agents" of the general public and then to ask how effectively the public, as "principals," use a country's political system to align the agents' actions with the public's interest. Does a cabinet minister, for example, feel effective pressure and demands from (or on behalf of) the public—from an expected opponent in the next election, say, or from an active media with access to budget data, or from a parliamentary scrutiny committee—to allocate education spending fairly and effectively to primary schools across the country? Alternatively, does the minister feel motivated—and at liberty—to concentrate resources on schools in certain politically favored districts or to divert funds into private pockets, because pressures for transparency and public accountability are weakly developed?

For the pathways of accountability described in chapter 3 to work requires that information on government budgets and financial management be readily available to citizens. Chapter 4 uses data from the Open Budget Initiative of the International Budget Partnership to show how to make budgets clear and transparent and how countries are falling short.

Because enforcing accountability on the government sector is a massive task, citizens cannot generally address it effectively as individuals. Interest has therefore grown in the role of intermediary civil society organizations that can act on behalf of the population to make governments more accountable. That role is a major focus of this book and is developed primarily in chapters 5 and 6. The focus is on independent monitoring organizations—civil society organizations whose mission is to monitor government policies and services and to demand more transparent and accountable performance in public expenditure management.

A critical focus—public expenditure management

Public spending in most low- and middle-income countries falls far short of being as effective or as equitably allocated as it needs to be. In the past donors and activists have focused on increasing the quantity of resources, including aid, for development-oriented programs. In recent years they have come to understand that improving the quality of public resource use can be at least as important.

World Bank research has found that the correlation between increased spending on public services and improved outcomes is often weak. Increased spending on education has not always resulted in higher primary school completion rates, and increased spending on health is only weakly associated with lower mortality rates in children under age 5. This suggests that increased public spending needs to be accompanied by more attention to the effective and efficient use of funds to achieve significant development impact.[1]

It is often observed that politicians can claim to be following almost any strategy to appease stakeholders such as international donors, other government leaders, and the public. But a government or ministry's true strategy and priorities are revealed by how it actually spends public money. In this spirit, and without diminishing the importance of other aspects of good governance such as respect for individual rights, this book focuses on "following the money."

Day to day, no area of government activity more directly affects development than public spending and service delivery. The public sector is often the primary provider of health and education services and the leading investor in infrastructure. The allocation of public spending may also be the key mechanism for income redistribution (whether progressive or regressive) across groups. Accordingly, budgets can determine how well or poorly scarce resources contribute to development goals. This book looks closely at how—and how far—the demand side, defined as pressures and demands coming from or on behalf of the public, can contribute to better public resource use and, ultimately, better development outcomes.

A growing literature explores the empirical relationship between government transparency and accountability for performance and the effectiveness of public expenditure management. These studies work from the hypothesis that increasing public knowledge of government processes and expanding opportunities for civil society to hold government accountable for its actions will increase administrators' incentives to allocate money and effort toward effective, propoor human and economic development programs. Box 1.1 highlights some of the most influential research in this area. While the research supports the notion that transparency can have a positive impact, more work is needed to define the mechanisms at play, including how demand-side agents, such as independent monitoring organizations, can improve development outcomes. The book focuses on independent monitoring organizations as a special breed of civil society organizations focused on public expenditures and service delivery performance.

Evolution of thinking on development and accountability

During the last 60 years mainstream thinking on the channels for achieving progress in economic and social development has evolved. The early post–World War II decades saw an emphasis on capital accumulation through increased savings and foreign aid, designed to move poor countries away from subsistence agriculture to more economically productive market-focused agriculture and manufacturing. By the 1980s emphasis was shifting to reforms in macroeconomic policies expected to improve economic performance, including fiscal stabilization, privatization, and trade liberalization. At the same time investment in people (through health, education, nutrition, and other programs) was being pursued more vigorously. By the late 20th century internationally supported programs for debt relief were adopting an explicit poverty-alleviation focus, conditioning debt relief on the development and implementation of national poverty reduction strategies.

Governance and the quality of public institutions

In parallel, a greater appreciation developed for the importance to successful development of country-level governance and the quality of public institutions—and

BOX 1.1

What do we know about the links between transparency, public expenditure, and human development?

Researchers have used micro-level country studies and cross-country studies to investigate links between transparency and the effectiveness of public spending. The micro studies focus on the role of the media in improving access to information, using media variables to proxy for transparency and measuring the effect on public spending. The cross-country studies use aggregated transparency indices to explain cross-country variation in human development indicators.

One of the first studies to use media to represent transparency employed a model of political transparency to show that government officials put more effort into propoor spending when the public has greater access to newspapers. Focusing on Federal Emergency Relief Act spending in the United States during the New Deal era, another study finds that an increase in the share of radio listeners was associated with an increase in funding, after controlling for differences in income levels across political units. A study on actual rather than allocated spending exploits a newspaper campaign in Uganda that allowed citizens to monitor a school grant program to test the hypothesis that districts with more access to the media have less corruption in the form of capture of public funds. The authors find that the public's and schools' access to information on education spending significantly reduced the capture of public school funds by local officials and politicians—from 80 percent in 1995 to less than 20 percent in 2001.

One of the few studies to explicitly investigate the link between transparency and development outcomes takes a cross-country approach. Creating a transparency index for 194 countries, the study finds that transparency is highly significant in explaining variation in human development indicators (including life expectancy, female literacy, and child immunization) across countries.

While research on transparency and human development is limited largely to the studies discussed above, a growing number of cross-country studies investigate the relationships between transparency, accountability, and the quality of governance. Although the studies do not extend their empirical analyses to development outcomes, much of the research is motivated by the assumption that good governance leads to advances in human development. A study of cross-country governance trends finds that transparency is positively and significantly correlated with many aspects of governance, including effectiveness, control of corruption, accountability, rule of law, and bureaucratic efficiency. The addition of variables measuring the extent of government ownership of media outlets weakens the impact of access to media on governance, suggesting that increased transparency is strongly associated with higher quality governance only to the extent that information is presented by sources independent of government.

Source: Besley and Burgess 2002; Stromberg 2004; Reinikka and Svensson 2004; Bellver and Kaufman 2005; Islam 2003.

the damage that can be done by widespread corruption. Improving governance has become increasingly prominent in international development discourse. In March 2007, for example, following extensive consultation, the World Bank approved a new strategy for promoting good governance.[2] In 2006 the United Kingdom's Department for International Development released a new antipoverty strategy that placed governance at the center of the organization's work program.[3] The U.S. Agency for International Development, the Inter-American Development Bank, and other leading development institutions have taken similar initiatives.[4]

Meanwhile, the increasing availability of comparable data on country-level governance standards has made it possible to study the empirical relationship between good governance and better development outcomes. The World Bank's Worldwide Governance Indicator, one of the most comprehensive governance indicators, accounts for six aspects of governance quality (voice and accountability, political stability and absence of violence, government effectiveness, regulatory quality, rule of law, and control of corruption). The index covers the recent period of governance reform (1996–2006). The latest analysis of the Worldwide Governance Indicator shows that while some improvements in governance have occurred in the past decade, they have been inconsistent across countries and dimensions of governance quality.[5] While indicators of integrity and corruption constructed by Global Integrity and Transparency International are not as telling on trends in governance, both provide additional evidence that governance quality varies greatly across regions and that poor governance continues to be an obstacle to poverty reduction and social development in many countries.[6]

Democratization and a new political landscape

As international development actors began focusing on improving governance and accountability, the political landscape in developing countries was shifting as well. There has been an unprecedented movement toward democratization since the 1980s, accelerated by the collapse of communism in Central and Eastern Europe and the discrediting of military rule in Latin America. The Polity Project of the University of Maryland defined 92 countries as democracies in 2007 and 30 as autocracies.[7]

Accompanying the trend toward political democracy has been a more general push for greater openness in society, greater adherence to the rule of law, more public participation in governance, and more emphasis on human rights. The Freedom in the World Index published annually by Freedom House seeks to capture these complementary trends. Its subcategories include electoral process, political pluralism, government functioning, freedom of expression, rule of law, and individual rights. According to its annual survey of political rights and civil liberties, the number of countries classified as "free" has risen from 43 to 89 in the past 30 years, while countries rated as "not free" have dropped by a third (from 39 percent of the total in 1981 to 24 percent of 194 countries in 2009). The same survey indicates that the number of electoral democracies rose from 66 in 1987 to 118 in 1996, although the total dropped to 116 by 2009. About 4.6 billion people lived under fully or partially democratic conditions in 2009, and 2.3 billion lived under "not free" conditions, with China alone accounting for about half that total. The trend toward democracy has been global, with every continent participating in the push for greater freedom and openness, although there have been setbacks and improvements year by year (with several serious setbacks just in the last few years).[8]

As this book argues, the potential for independent monitoring organizations to affect public spending varies, depending in large part on how much political space is available in which to operate. In newly democratic societies civil society is potentially well placed to improve accountability and governance. The stakes in holding governments accountable for their decisions are especially large in public expenditure management: public spending priorities and implementation affect daily life. The recent trend toward democratization means that civil society can develop the voice, power, and tools to influence government decisions and actions in developing countries, fundamentally altering the dynamic of policy reform by shifting the center of decisionmaking to domestic players.

The role of external agents

Not yet well understood is how outside organizations—donors, capacity-building organizations, and others—can contribute to greater domestic demand for good governance. The idea itself, at least on the surface, is somewhat paradoxical. Can outsiders really create domestic demand for good governance? Should they even try? For more than 50 years the democracy-building community—largely centered in the U.S. State Department but including organizations such as the National Democratic Institute, the International Republican Institute, and International IDEA—has worked on issues related to this goal. Their experience may provide some useful models and strategies for increasing and broadening citizen control of governments, but that experience also offers warnings about the difficulty of achieving success. This book investigates a range of strategies for outside organizations to support civil society's demand for greater accountability for results in public spending.

A simple model

Figure 1.1 offers a framework for thinking about the key relationships explored in this book. At the top the goal is to achieve *better development outcomes*. From the bottom a combination of *supply-side improvements*, such as enforcing anticorruption

FIGURE 1.1

A model of governance, public expenditure management, and the role of independent monitoring organizations

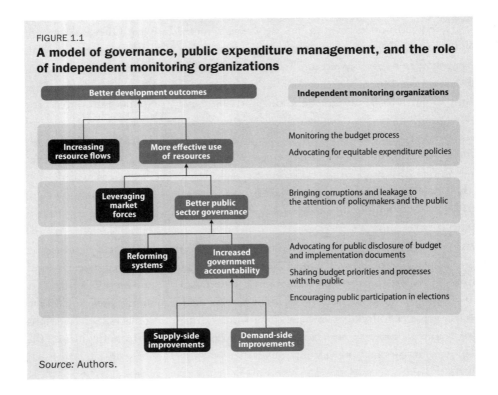

Source: Authors.

laws, and *demand-side improvements*, such as developing independent monitoring organizations, is probably necessary to create enduring *improvements in government accountability*, the next step up the chain. Greater accountability creates an environment where another supply-side intervention, *reforming systems,* is likely to have a tangible impact. For example, improving government accountability in procurement by making it transparent, standardizing and simplifying procedures, and creating an arbitration process to settle problems quickly gives citizens and bidders the ability to demand that the system perform better. The government may then begin forcefully prosecuting criminal behavior, upgrading information systems, and removing layers of bureaucrats built up over time whose job was to enforce accountability through processes. This combination leads to *better public sector governance*, with the result that public procurement becomes faster and more trustworthy. More trustworthy procurement opens possibilities to develop contracts and competitive processes for service delivery, thus *leveraging market forces* to make *more effective use of resources.* Now *increased resource flows* can be expected to actually have an impact. To the far right of the figure are some of the actions that independent monitoring organizations could take at each stage to improve accountability.

The balance of this chapter explores in greater detail the stages outlined in figure 1.1.

Achieving better development outcomes requires change

Figure 1.1 starts from the proposition that the objective of government efforts should be the pursuit of better development outcomes—the rationale behind the urgency to reform governance in many countries (see box 1.2 on Peru). But what does "better outcomes" mean?

Some analysts give primacy to a country's overall rate of economic growth, while others emphasize measures that reflect distributional aspects—such as poverty incidence or measures of inequality such as the Gini coefficient. Most reviews extend beyond purely economic indicators to take in physical measures of welfare, such as literacy rates or life expectancy.

One measure of success is the Millennium Development Goals, which provide a scorecard, officially recognized by governments and development institutions, of countries' effectiveness in meeting the needs of their people.[9] Anyone interested in development progress in specific countries or on specific issues now has ready access to annually updated performance data.[10] The United Nations produces a flagship annual report assessing progress and the remaining challenges,[11] and other development institutions publish complementary publications.

The picture is uneven. There has been considerable progress in some areas. Most notably, the proportion of people living in extreme poverty fell from nearly a

---

BOX 1.2
Introducing results-based budgeting in Peru

Responding to the Peruvian government's interest in results-based budgeting, the Research Center at the Universidad del Pacífico (CIUP) conducted a study of the country's record of public spending and outcomes in health and education. The study would provide a baseline against which to measure the success of the new initiative and recommendations for moving forward with performance-based budgeting. Using subnational indicators such as maternal health, infant mortality, and school performance, CIUP found that past budget allocations reflected neither the needs nor the relative development outcomes of different regions. In presenting these findings to key government officials, CIUP emphasized the importance of results-based budgeting in a country that needs to improve its measures of social development. At the same time, CIUP questioned how much impact results-based budgeting would have if it were adopted without complementary strengthening of incentives for public employees to improve performance and to deliver against the results-based expenditure system.

Source: Alvarado and Morón 2007.

third to less than a fifth between 1990 and 2004.[12] Progress has also been made in boosting primary enrollment, improving gender equality, reducing child mortality, and controlling certain diseases, including malaria and tuberculosis.[13] At the same time, however, the number of women who die from treatable and preventable complications of pregnancy and childbirth, the number of malnourished children, and the number of people without basic sanitation all remain far from target levels. Progress has been uneven across countries and regions, with some areas showing little or no progress against many of the goals.

Despite the bright spots, then, many countries have not yet met the Millennium Development Goal targets. According to *World Development Indicators 2009*, an estimated 1.4 billion people still live in extreme poverty (on less than $1.25 a day) and 2.6 billion people live in poverty (less than $2 a day).[14] We cannot rely on time alone to change this: too many lives hang in the balance. That is why the issues discussed in this book matter.

Focusing on effective use of resources

The second theme in figure 1.1 is the importance of more effective use of resources (see box 1.3 for Kenya's experience with education grants). Self-evidently, waste, inefficiency, and the diversion of resources from their intended goals impede the pursuit of development goals.

The debate on whether developing countries need more resources or need to use existing resources better misses the real issue. The two are not always alternatives—many countries, especially the poorest, could no doubt benefit from both. Current levels of aid are well below the target of 0.7 percent of donor countries' GDP set by the United Nations in 1970.[15] In 2006 overall official development assistance, at $103.9 billion, was 5.1 percent below the total in 2005 and just 0.30 percent of Development Assistance Committee member countries' combined gross national income—less than half the UN target.[16] If these countries provided aid at the 0.7 percent level, the total would be about $242.4 billion. It seems reasonable to expect that many development challenges could be addressed more effectively with an additional $140 billion a year.

Aid levels ultimately reflect the outcome of domestic political processes within donor countries. These countries face many competing demands on their resources. The case for a larger overseas aid program is undermined if donor country voters believe that waste, inefficiency, fraud, and corruption are widespread in the public sectors of aid-recipient countries. But if developing country aid recipients can achieve more efficient use of existing resources, this can strengthen the case for additional resources.

BOX 1.3
Improving the effectiveness of education spending in Kenya

The government of Kenya sought to improve education opportunities for the poorest and most vulnerable groups through the Secondary Education Bursary Scheme, which provides grants to students for secondary school tuition and fees. The Institute for Policy Analysis and Research in Nairobi wanted to determine whether the program was being targeted in ways that effectively increased the number of poor Kenyans completing secondary education. The researchers discovered that the officials allocating the grants were opting for quantity over quality, providing a large number of students with the minimum award level—an amount that did not cover the cost of a single full year of school. Interviews indicated that many students were unable to cover fees, even with the help of a program grant, and thus were forced to drop out of school. The researchers recommended that the total funding level of the program be increased and, in a recommendation that policymakers might find easier to adopt, that students receiving a grant in their first year of secondary school be given a commitment of funding that would allow them to complete all four years, subject to adequate performance.

Source: Kibua and others 2008.

However compelling the arguments for increased levels of aid, developing countries cannot afford to wait for some hoped-for windfall of additional financing to assist them in fulfilling their development goals. They must make more out of the resources already available. And more robust systems for expenditure management will make additional aid feasible by allowing donors to channel funds through government systems with greater confidence. More money is needed and will help, but better performance is essential for deriving greater impact from existing resources, particularly from developing countries' own funds. The role of aid is often overemphasized. Even the poorest countries use domestic resources to finance high proportions of education and health budgets—two areas of special interest to donors.

Improving public sector governance
The next element in the logical chain in figure 1.1 is the need to improve the quality of public sector governance to achieve systematic improvement in the use of resources. The findings of the Bandung Institute in Indonesia suggest that better public sector governance can have a significant impact on the quality of social sector services (box 1.4).

It is not necessary to become embroiled in a debate about public or private provision of services to make the point that both require better governance. *World Development Report 2004: Making Services Work for Poor People* characterized

BOX 1.4
Better outcomes with better governance in Indonesia

The results of a study of public expenditure allocations in the Indonesian health and education systems by the Bandung Institute of Governance Studies showed that national, provincial, and municipal governments fell far short of allocating the legally required minimums of 20 percent of the budget to education and 15 percent to health. More detailed analysis of public expenditures at the local level showed great variation in the quality of budget management. Some subnational government officials had developed innovative solutions to public health and education problems, including free services at community health centers and schools. The study found evidence that the innovations in public spending could be attributed to strong policymakers and better quality governance. The availability of funds to pay for these innovations was directly related to localities' ability to hold down the share of salary costs in their budgets. The variability in spending, approaches, and apparent effectiveness in a small geographic area shows the impact reformers can have.

Source: BIGS 2008.

traditional government provision as requiring the "long route of accountability," whereas competitive forces allow for a "short route of accountability," meaning accountability to citizens and users of services.[17]

There are many examples of successful private sector involvement in service provision around the world. Some public services lend themselves well to competitive market provision. The transformation of worldwide telecommunications sectors, once dominated by public monopolies, into competitive, privately operated businesses is one example. In many parts of the developing world religious organizations have long worked alongside the public sector in providing primary, secondary, and sometimes tertiary education. In South Asia well more than 80 percent of health spending is out-of-pocket spending by patients in private markets. Nongovernment schools are common everywhere, usually serving elites.

But such examples do not obviate the need for strong public sector governance. Government officials occupy a key level in any chain of service provision, whether civil servants are acting as frontline service providers, policymakers are selecting private contractors to fulfill these roles, or the executive is deciding how much to allocate to education and health (and for whom). In fact, greater use of the "short route of accountability" places demands on governments in areas where they have often performed poorly—procurement, contract management, and monitoring and evaluation. Without constant improvements in governance, service provision is likely to continue to fail especially those groups that depend most on the government to pay for or deliver services.

Increasing government accountability is an essential complement to reforming systems

The next stage of the argument in figure 1.1 is that the key requirement for achieving improved standards of public sector governance is more accountability for those working in the public sector. (The nature and sources of accountability are explored in greater detail in chapter 3.) There are multiple routes to achieving accountability (see box 1.5 for an example from Paraguay). In a hierarchical bureaucracy the performance of individual civil servants depends on the success of their supervisors in enforcing internal "vertical" accountability for performance. Military performance depends heavily on discipline in following orders, for example. But what about the accountability of those at the top of the hierarchy, whether senior civil servants or politicians? Who can hold them accountable for acting in the public interest? One of the thrusts of this book is that, at some stage, effective public sector accountability needs to include accountability to the public, enforced by a variety of mechanisms—such as elections, checks and balances, and the functioning of civil society intermediaries.

As used by the international development community, the term *governance reform* covers a wide and diverse range of interventions. If governance is viewed simply as how governments manage their administrative systems and exercise their power, almost any governmental reform can be described as a governance reform. Donors fund governance reforms that range from installing new computer

---

BOX 1.5

Increasing budgetary transparency in Paraguay

With Paraguay's recent democratization, the Center for Economic Analysis and Dissemination in Paraguay (CADEP) set out to investigate how efficiently the government was spending money on primary school students in the capital city of Asunción. It found that a lack of transparency and accountability in social sector spending remained despite the fall of the dictatorship. Because of the lack of data, CADEP had to rely on interviews and qualitative evidence of corruption rather than track funds from source to facility as it had planned to do. Researchers concluded that budgeting is too opaque to be monitored by civil society. However, as CADEP began disseminating the evidence that it was able to collect, it found an active and enthusiastic audience for the work—parent associations. Developing a creative poster project and targeted participatory action plans with parent associations and school officials, CADEP has paved a way forward for increasing the transparency of budgeting in education and making it feasible for civil society to monitor at least certain aspects of government performance in this sector.

Source: Brizuela Speratti 2008.

systems to sending judges to observe the judiciary in other countries and building new courts, as well as technical assistance to streamline procurement procedures and much more. Improving and professionalizing a country's system for selecting, incentivizing, controlling, and replacing civil servants is an important reform that has a narrow mechanical focus.

Such governance reforms go only part of the way and are probably not sufficient to spur fundamental improvements. Such reforms often do not address the root problem of managing and monitoring policymakers and the government unit in which they function. Unless politicians and civil servants believe that they will be held accountable for their decisions and actions, government reforms cannot change the incentives that policymakers face and thus will have a limited impact on the effectiveness and equity of public spending.

The goal of increasing government accountability serves as an obvious focus for civil society, in particular for independent monitoring organizations. Members of civil society benefit or suffer from the expenditure decisions and actions of the government. Further, the public is well placed to monitor the public expenditure chain and to make its opinions heard (particularly during elections) on how public resources are used.

A core theme of this book is that institutional reforms, competition among countries to improve government systems and the regulatory environment, outside help from international organizations and bilateral donors, and other mechanisms may all be useful in public sector reform. They are, however, generally insufficient for gaining lasting improvements, which requires active domestic voices that demand change.

Supporting and motivating demand-side interventions

Budget management reforms initiated by international development institutions have often not been completed, not gone far enough, or been reversed at the first opportunity. Indeed, despite extensive reform efforts, public expenditure management remains weak in much of the developing world. (Chapter 2 takes a more in-depth look at public expenditure management systems and institutions around the world.)

What seems clear is that a new dynamism is needed to catalyze further progress on public sector reform. That dynamism is most readily available in the potential of independent monitoring organizations to become champions of change in the public expenditure arena (see box 1.6 for an example in Ghana). Chapter 3 presents a conceptual framework for considering how demand-side agents can improve government accountability, public sector governance, and resource allocation.

BOX 1.6
Shaping the dialogue on education spending in Ghana

Recognizing that one of the biggest causes of waste in education spending is teacher absenteeism, the Center for Democratic Development (CDD) in Ghana sought to estimate the incidence of absenteeism among primary school teachers. CDD researchers identified long-distance travel by teachers to education courses as a common cause of absenteeism. They also proposed a feasible solution: move teacher training courses from Friday afternoon to Saturday. More broadly, the CDD's positive reputation with the media, and the fact that the researchers were on the ground for the full run-up to the 2008 presidential and parliamentary elections, meant that CDD was able to help shape dialogue and debate on how to make Ghanaian education spending more efficient and less wasteful. As a result of the CDD's work, the Ghana Education Service is working on making concrete policy changes to remove common causes of teacher absenteeism.

Source: CDD 2008.

Chapter 4 then looks at what transparency and accountability mean for budgets and expenditure management and at the weak mechanisms for monitoring and evaluating outcomes. Chapters 3 and 4 lay out the theory and the challenges, then chapter 5 provides examples of the impact that independent monitoring organizations can have on public expenditure practices and of specific interventions that demand-side agents can take to affect each stage of the process shown in figure 1.1.

The final piece of the puzzle is how the international donor community can support development of this capability. Chapter 6 outlines ways in which multilateral organizations, bilateral aid agencies, private donors, and civil society organizations can nurture the development of independent monitoring organizations. Money and other types of support matter, of course, but many other things can be done to help mainstream independent monitoring organizations by engaging them as partners and extending the supply-side agenda on governance with a view to opening up the books of government spending—a necessary condition for the development and effectiveness of independent monitoring organizations. Chapter 7 then looks at what all the key players—donors, governments, and independent monitoring organizations—can do to strengthen independent monitoring organizations and increase their impact.

A word of caution on a promising agenda

This book presents some evidence of the strides made by civil society in improving development outcomes and recommendations for supporting these organizations moving forward. However, demand-side interventions in governance and public expenditure management are only one piece of the solution and not a panacea for achieving development goals.

Although the recent democratization trend has touched all regions of the world, many countries continue to be governed by authoritarian regimes with no formal avenues for civil society to influence policymaking. Governance systems and the extent of political freedom largely determine the scope that independent monitoring organizations have to hold policymakers accountable for their decisions. Consider Peru, a country that qualifies as free based on Freedom House rankings (and, indeed, ranks above developed countries such as Sweden in budget openness, according to the International Budget Project's Open Budget Index[18]). Peru has shown great innovation in its public expenditure practices, implementing results-based budgeting in recent years, and has created many entry points for organizations such as the Research Center at the Universidad del Pacífico (CIUP) to enter the policy debate and influence stakeholders (see box 1.2). But the success of organizations like CIUP depends on a degree of transparency so that independent monitoring organizations can have access to information on public expenditures. Countries lacking some minimal degree of transparency may not offer such obvious scope for a civil society role in the budget dialogue. Timely and inexpensive access to understandable information is a necessary precondition for bottom-up accountability.

Even in countries where civil society is well placed to analyze public spending decisions and advocate for improvements in public expenditures and services, independent monitoring organizations can face other obstacles, particularly problems of capabilities and absorption. Problems of capabilities include challenges that result from a lack of resources or abilities within the organization, such as inadequate technical expertise to conduct budget analyses, difficulty retaining skilled team members, and lack of an appropriate communications strategy. Problems of absorption reflect inadequate support by external forces in assisting independent monitoring organizations in their work or a lack of receptiveness to the dissemination and advocacy efforts of civil society. Challenges of this type include governments withholding public expenditure information from citizens or being unwilling to meet with independent monitoring organization representatives to discuss their results and policy recommendations.

Finally, success depends on a combination of complementary elements. For example, strong think tanks might be able to uncover evidence of fraud or waste, but without an effective and independent news media, they may not be able to communicate their findings. And if the information is successfully disseminated, are there mechanisms through which citizens can act to achieve change? Often analytical organizations have little interest in lobbying to fix problems, and advocacy organizations have little use for careful analysis. An independent monitoring organization needs to be a hybrid of both.

Notes

1. World Bank (2003c) provides an extensive review of the weak relationship between public spending and development outcomes.
2. World Bank 2006b.
3. DFID 2006.
4. USAID 2005; IDB 2004.
5. Kaufmann, Kraay, and Mastruzzi 2007.
6. Global Integrity 2008; Transparency International 2009.
7. See Polity IV Database (www.sytemicpeace.org/polity/polity4.htm). The Polity Project is one of the activities of the Center for International Development and Conflict Management. The database contains information on regime and authority characteristics for all countries with populations of more than 500,000 and covers the period 1800–2007.
8. Freedom House 2010.
9. United Nations General Assembly 2000.
10. www.mdgmonitor.org
11. United Nations 2007, p. 1.
12. United Nations 2007, p. 4
13. United Nations 2007, p. 4.
14. World Bank 2009b.
15. www.oecd.org/document/17/0,2340,en_2649_33721_38341265_1_1_1_1,00.html.
16. Sachs 2005.
17. World Bank 2003d, p. 6.
18. IBP/OBI 2009.

Major issues and tools in public expenditure management

Your budget decisions really show your policy priorities. You can say your priority is poverty, but it's your budget decision that shows whether that priority is matched by spending.

—Hon. Pregs Govender, South African Member of Parliament[1]

This chapter summarizes the main issues in public expenditure in low- and middle-income countries based on roughly 60 public expenditure reviews conducted by the World Bank between 2000 and 2007. The World Bank has been conducting public expenditure reviews for low- and middle-income countries since the 1980s, analyzing the level and pattern of public expenditure, assessing the effectiveness and equity of public spending, and identifying bottlenecks to improved spending effectiveness. The reviews have provided valuable insights to guide policy dialogue and have frequently resulted in tangible fiscal reform in many countries.

Countries need a strategic approach to expenditure planning

A recurring theme in public expenditure reviews is the weak relationship between a country's strategic goals and its national budget. Although budget preparation is usually an elaborate exercise involving multiple government ministries and departments, it is often driven more by inertia than by strategic thinking. There is excessive reliance on input-oriented (or line-item) budgeting of inputs such as staff, travel, and supplies and little attention to how the overall budget allocation will advance national goals.[2] Ministries and departments often decide on the level of increase to be applied to the main expenditure items in their budget. The sectoral objectives often boil down to seeking as many resources as possible instead of ensuring that available resources are used more effectively to address policy goals. These problems are by no means unique to poorer countries, but they pose particular threats in resource-poor environments.

The preoccupation with inputs coincides with an underemphasis on outputs and outcomes. Few countries systematically evaluate the effectiveness of public services, the effect of increased public spending on the delivery of quality public services, and the impact of public expenditure on poverty and social outcomes.[3] The lack of rigorous evaluation means that policymakers do not readily learn from mistakes.

This budget formulation process makes it difficult for the budget to serve as a policy tool for furthering the government's growth, poverty, and social objectives. The lack of evaluation means that government agencies cannot be held accountable for their budget allocations or their performance.[4]

One country that has linked its policy goals to its budget allocations better than many is South Africa. South Africa has a rolling policy framework—embodied in a set of rolling priorities—that is updated annually, rather than national strategic plans that are formulated only occasionally. These rolling policy priorities are closely connected to government spending, with each informing the other. The priorities are derived from a broad set of development mandates, many drawn from the Bill of Rights in the South African Constitution.[5] South Africa's policy- and budget-making process is consultative and part of a vibrant national debate that includes a robust free media and an engaged civil society.

The government's role is often too broad to be successful

Another overarching issue is what governments *should* be spending their money on. A recurring problem is the large amount of public spending on inessential activities (such as running commercially oriented public enterprises).[6] If such functions can be shed or reduced, the size of government can be matched to the resources available. The remaining public functions can then focus on advancing the government's strategic agenda.

Pakistan illustrates this predicament. The legislative framework and the Constitution subscribe to the notion of fiscal federalism, but in practice the federal government has expanded into areas of shared responsibility, into functions assigned constitutionally to subnational governments, and into functions traditionally performed by the private sector.[7]

Pakistan is not unique. Many governments spend scarce public resources on subsidies to loss-making state-owned enterprises. In Zambia, one of the most heavily indebted countries, the overall public sector (quasi-fiscal) deficit is estimated at 14–18 percent of GDP, nearly 40 percent of it accounted for by losses of state-owned corporations.[8] In Kenya, transfers to state enterprises siphoned off 11–12 percent of public expenditure in 2002/03 and 2003/04.[9] In Swaziland in 2004/05 subsidies to public enterprises were almost equal to the country's total recurrent public spending on health—meaning that without those subsidies public expenditure on health could have been doubled.

Spending tends to be inefficient and inequitable

Efficiency refers to the allocation of public expenditure across uses to obtain the maximum output from the allocated spending. Equity refers to how benefits from public spending are distributed across income segments of the population. If a disproportionate share of the benefits goes to the better-off sections of society, who typically constitute a small share of the population, public spending is considered inequitable and not propoor.

It is not straightforward to compare returns to public spending across sectors, as many sectors produce goods and services that are not readily marketable and are therefore difficult to value. In addition, there are externalities (effects outside the sector) associated with certain types of public spending that complicate estimation of returns to spending in a single sector. Estimates of the broad returns from investing in various sectors are too tenuous for policy formulation and budget allocation.

It is sometimes easier to compare returns across types of public spending within a single sector. For instance, there is empirical research that establishes that the returns (both private and social) to primary levels of schooling are greater than those to higher levels (table 2.1).[10] Likewise, there is plenty of evidence that government expenditure on public health activities, such as communicable disease control and disease prevention, has higher social returns than spending on curative care.[11]

Public expenditure on primary education is also decidedly propoor. The poor tend to have more primary school–age children than the nonpoor do, and poor children are more likely to attend public primary schools than are better-off children. Also, children from poor households are much less likely than those from high-income households to enroll in secondary school or higher education. Public spending on primary health care is also typically much more propoor than is spending on secondary and tertiary care for much the same reasons: the poor are more likely than the better-off to use public primary health care facilities and are less likely to access secondary or tertiary care. Thus, spending on elementary education and primary health care advance both efficiency and equity goals relative to spending on secondary and tertiary education and health services.

TABLE 2.1
Average estimated rates of return to schooling, by region, 1990s (percent)

Region	Social rates of return to schooling			Private rates of return to schooling		
	Primary	Secondary	Higher	Primary	Secondary	Higher
Sub-Saharan Africa	25.4	18.4	11.3	37.6	24.6	27.8
Asia	16.2	11.1	11.0	20.0	15.8	18.2
Europe, Middle East & North Africa	15.6	9.7	9.9	13.8	13.6	18.8
Latin America & Caribbean	17.4	12.9	12.3	26.6	17.0	19.5
High-income countries	8.5	9.4	8.5	13.4	11.3	11.6
World	18.9	13.1	10.8	26.6	17.9	19.0

Source: Psacharopoulos and Patrinos 2002.

TABLE 2.2
Benefit incidence of public spending by income quintile, selected countries, 1990s (percent)

Country	Share of public spending accruing to					Year
	Poorest	Second	Third	Fourth	Richest	
Health						
Chile	32	26	21	15	6	1992
Colombia	27	26	19	16	13	1992
Indonesia	12	16	19	24	29	1990
Romania	12	15	20	24	29	1994
Primary education						
Argentina	37	23	15	15	9	1993
Chile	36	27	18	13	7	1990
Colombia	39	26	19	11	4	1992
Guyana	29	25	19	19	9	1992
Pakistan	19	23	22	21	15	1991
Secondary education						
Argentina	22	21	21	21	15	1993
Chile	24	24	21	18	13	1990
Colombia	21	27	25	18	10	1992
Indonesia	5	11	17	26	42	1989
Romania	18	22	22	21	18	1994

Source: Davoodi, Sachjapinan, and Kim 2001; De Mello 2004.

Yet public spending in many countries is skewed toward higher levels of schooling and health care (table 2.2). Public expenditures tend to be more propoor in Latin America (Argentina, Chile, and Colombia) than in Asia (Indonesia and Pakistan). Across all countries, public spending on health care and primary education is decidedly more propoor than is public spending on secondary education. In Indonesia, for example, 68 percent of public spending on secondary education benefits the richest 40 percent of the population, while 16 percent benefits the poorest 40 percent.

There is some evidence from Ecuador on which public programs tend to be the most propoor (table 2.3). For instance, the poorest 20 percent of the population benefits from more than a third of public spending on primary schools and school breakfasts but only 3 percent of spending on universities, while the richest 20 percent of the population benefits from 41 percent of public spending on universities. The subsidies on gasoline (abolished in 2003), social security–based health spending, and cooking gas are not propoor. Overall, the poorest 20 percent of the population receives 17.4 percent of all government social outlays, compared with 21.4 percent for the richest 20 percent. In 2003 the most propoor program, school breakfast, received an annual allocation of less than 1 percent of total social spending. In contrast, university education, one of the most regressive social subsidies, accounted for nearly 20 percent of social spending. Likewise, the propoor Rural Social Security spending on health care received only one-fifth of the government resources that went to the non-propoor Ecuadorian Social Security Institute health care program.

Mongolia is another low-income country with a lopsided distribution of public spending. Mongolia suffers from high rates of infant mortality and a high burden of communicable diseases. Yet much of its public spending goes to hospital-based services that are neither propoor nor public health oriented. In 2000 general and specialized hospitals received more than two-thirds of the national health budget.[12] Likewise, in Kenya just two tertiary-level hospitals accounted for 18 percent of all recurrent public expenditure on health in 2002/03.[13] Overall, 68 percent of recurrent public health spending went to curative services.[14]

By contrast, in Bangladesh, another low-income country, budgetary expenditures are broadly consistent with its economic and social development goals, especially in human development, disaster management, and agricultural development. In particular, the government has maintained a strategic balance in its public expenditures on education. As in other low-income countries, however, public spending on primary education is decidedly propoor, while public spending on tertiary education largely benefits the better-off groups (table 2.4).

TABLE 2.3

Incidence of social expenditure and energy subsidies in Ecuador by income quintile, 1999 (percent unless otherwise indicated)

← Less propoor expenditure   More propoor expenditure →

Item	Gasoline subsidy	University tuition	Health care Social Security institute	Cooking gas	Secondary school	Health care Ministry of Health	Health care Rural Social Security	Bono (social insurance)	Primary school	School breakfast
Income quintile										
Poorest	0	3	5	8	15	19	26	27	35	38
Second	1	12	7	14	23	23	35	28	26	15
Third	4	16	21	20	22	22	13	25	20	12
Fourth	10	28	22	24	24	24	21	16	13	33
Richest	85	41	45	34	14	12	5	4	6	2
Government social expenditures										
Amount (2003 $ millions)		366.4	191.4	221.0	304.0	160.2	35.9	159.9	453.4	17.0
Share of total (percent)		19.2	10.0	11.6	15.9	8.4	1.9	8.4	23.7	0.9

Source: World Bank 2004a.

TABLE 2.4

Benefit incidence of public expenditure on education in Bangladesh, by consumption expenditure quintile, 2000 (percent)

Level of education	Poorest	Second	Third	Fourth	Richest
Primary education	22	23	22	19	14
Secondary	6	11	16	28	40
Tertiary	6	6	10	21	57
All education	12	15	17	23	32

Source: World Bank 2003c.

In the early 1990s primary schools received nearly half of Bangladesh's recurrent education expenditure (table 2.5). Primary enrollment rose sharply during the 1990s, reaching near-universal enrollment by the mid-1990s. The large increase in primary enrollments during the early 1990s began generating increased demand for secondary education. As a result, spending on secondary education increased steadily through the 1990s. But even by 1999/2000, 40 percent of recurrent

TABLE 2.5

Recurrent public expenditure on education in Bangladesh, by level, 1991/92–1999/2000 (percent)

Fiscal year	Share of GDP	Distribution of recurrent public expenditure on education				
		Primary	Secondary	Technical	University	Other
1991/92	1.14	48.5	36.8	2.4	8.5	3.7
1993/94	1.30	47.0	41.1	2.2	7.9	1.8
1996/97	1.30	43.5	42.9	2.1	7.9	3.6
1998/99	1.35	40.4	47.6	1.4	7.0	3.7
1999/2000	1.37	39.5	48.4	1.4	8.0	2.7

Source: World Bank 2003c.

education spending went to primary education. The government struck a successful partnership with the private sector and nongovernmental organizations in expanding secondary school enrollments.

Bangladesh also provides a telling example of how inefficiencies in service delivery can prevent the poor from benefiting fully from propoor programs. For instance, the country's two main development programs—Vulnerable Group Development and Food for Work—are well targeted, with the poorest 20 percent of the population more than three times as likely to participate as the richest 20 percent. However, while the allocation of expenditures in these programs is broadly propoor, the benefits that the poor receive fall short of intentions. In this case, the weak links in the process are the service delivery institutions, which remain mired in bureaucratic inefficiencies and corruption.[15]

Underfunding nonsalary expenses

Another measure of efficiency is internal efficiency, or the combination of inputs allocated to produce outputs or outcomes within a sector. Overuse of one input relative to others is generally inefficient. Of course, determining the most efficient combination of inputs to produce a given output is difficult a priori. However, if 90 percent of recurrent spending in, say, education goes to teacher salaries, it can be inferred that other important education inputs, such as textbooks, instructional materials, and student scholarships, are underfunded. Several public expenditure reviews suggest that there is ample scope in low- and middle-income countries to improve internal efficiency by reducing the high share of salaries and wages in public expenditure and increasing the share of nonsalary inputs.

The weak funding of nonsalary expenses is widespread in the education sector. In China, for instance, only 7–9 percent of budgetary expenditures on education go to nonsalary items. In some provinces, such as Hezheng and Jishishan, wages and salaries absorb 93–98 percent of recurrent expenditures in education.[16] As a result, schools are run-down and lack instructional materials.

The situation in Sub-Saharan Africa is no different (table 2.6). In Burundi, for instance, salaries account for 99.6 percent of recurrent expenditure on primary education. Eritrea, Ghana, South Africa, Swaziland, Zambia, and Zimbabwe all allocate more than 90 percent of public spending on primary education to salaries. What this means is that parents are expected to pay for everything else, including textbooks and supplies.

One reason for the high share of salary costs in recurrent education spending is the political pressure in many low- and middle-income countries to hire more teachers than are needed for government schools. Teachers are civil servants, and the civil service is seen as an employer of first resort. For instance, Uzbekistan has a lower student-teacher (or higher teacher-student) ratio than many Organisation for Economic Co-operation and Development (OECD) countries (table 2.7), an inefficient use of education resources. There are, of course, large variations in the student-teacher ratio across developing countries. Within Sub-Saharan Africa, the primary school student-teacher ratio varies from 26 in Cape Verde to 72 in Ethiopia.[17]

The high ratio of wages and salaries in nonrecurrent public spending is not restricted to education. Many governments find it difficult to restrict growth in public employment, thus squeezing out allocations to nonwage operations and

TABLE 2.6

Primary school salary costs as a share of recurrent expenditure on primary education, selected Sub-Saharan African countries, 2002–04 (percent)

Country	Share (percent)
Burundi	99.6
Ghana	98.2
Zimbabwe	97.6
Eritrea	97.2
South Africa	95.9
Zambia	95.3
Swaziland	93.6
Togo	85.6
Seychelles	84.9
Lesotho	75.6
Comoros	65.5

Source: World Bank 2006c.

TABLE 2.7
Student-teacher ratios by level of education, selected countries, circa 2000

Country	Preschool	Primary	Lower secondary	Upper secondary	Higher
Uzbekistan	11.0	18.0	13.0	15.0	12.0
Korea, Rep.	23.9	32.2	21.9	22.5	—
United Kingdom	16.5	22.5	17.4	12.4	18.5
United States	19.3	16.3	16.8	14.5	14.0
OECD average	15.4	18.0	15.2	14.1	15.3

—is not available.
Source: World Bank 2005d.

maintenance. In Ecuador, for instance, the real rate of growth of the public payroll was 21 percent in 2001, 35 percent in 2002, and 20 percent in 2003. Not surprisingly, the share of current expenditure going to wages and salaries almost doubled during this period, rising from 25 percent in 2000 to 45 percent in 2003.

High salaries for teachers are another reason for the large share of salary expenses in recurrent public spending on education. (Of course, very low teacher salaries can lead to low morale, less teacher commitment to their jobs, and widespread teacher absenteeism.) The United Nations Educational, Scientific, and Cultural Organization (UNESCO) suggests that, on average for countries seeking to reach the Education for All targets, a reasonable level for an average primary school teacher's salary would be 3.5 times a country's per capita GDP.[18] Teacher salaries tend to be high in Sub-Saharan Africa (table 2.8). In Burkina Faso and Ethiopia, primary school teachers are paid salaries that are eight or more times per capita GDP. The multiples are more reasonable in Malawi and Tanzania, suggesting that this problem can be managed.

Overreliance on subsidies

Many of the most wasteful and regressive subsidies go to state-owned enterprises and utilities. And often these subsidies constitute a large share of a country's total subsidy bill. In Armenia, for instance, subsidies in the form of accumulated debt and tax arrears of utilities were estimated at 6–7.5 percent of GDP in 1996–2002.[19] Sometimes, the subsidies are implicit and are not reflected in the budget. In Iran, for instance, energy (electricity, gas, kerosene, and gasoline) is the most heavily subsidized item, with an implicit subsidy as high as 11 percent of GDP during the 1990s.[20]

Such implicit and explicit subsidies are regressive, consuming scarce public resources that could be used more efficiently to provide targeted social assistance.

TABLE 2.8

Primary school teacher salaries as a multiple of GDP per capita, selected developing countries, circa 2000

Country	Ratio
Bangladesh	5.3
Burkina Faso	8.0
Ethiopia	8.1
Malawi	4.0
Tanzania	3.6

Source: World Bank 2004c, p. 42.

For instance, it is estimated that the poor in rural areas in Iran receive only 11 percent of the energy subsidies; the share for the urban poor is even smaller, at 6 percent (table 2.9).[21]

In Ecuador, subsidies to basic services—water, telecommunications, and electricity—are a major part of public expenditure, accounting for 1.3 percent of GDP. These subsidies are economically inefficient,[22] and they fail to benefit the poor. The subsidy for telephone service is the most unequally distributed, with almost half of it going to the richest 20 percent but just 5 percent going to the poorest 20 percent (table 2.10). The three subsidies benefit the top 20 percent three times more than they do the bottom 20 percent.[23]

Most developing countries have substantially reduced the share of general price subsidies in public expenditure over the last decade or so. In China the government gradually reduced subsidies to state-owned enterprises even as the number of loss-making enterprises continued to grow through the 1990s. Spending on all subsidies fell from 27 percent of budgetary expenditure in 1986 to 7 percent by 1998, while spending on enterprise loss subsidies fell from 9.2 percent to 3.3 percent.[24]

TABLE 2.9

Share of selected subsidies accruing to the poor and nonpoor in Iran, 1998 (percent)

Subsidized item	Rural poor	Rural nonpoor	Urban poor	Urban nonpoor
Energy	11	89	6	94
Wheat	10	91	6	94
Pharmaceuticals	18	82	3	97
Edible oil and sugar	13	87	8	92

Source: World Bank 2005c, p. 45.

TABLE 2.10

Benefit incidence of subsidies on basic services in Ecuador, by consumption expenditure quintile, 2003 (percent)

Subsidy	Poorest	Second	Third	Fourth	Richest
Electricity	8.4	12.0	16.4	23.4	39.8
Water	7.9	12.0	15.2	23.6	41.3
Telephone	5.0	9.0	13.0	25.0	48.0
All three	7.3	11.2	15.0	23.9	42.6

Source: World Bank 2003c.

Once provided, subsidies are difficult to remove without arousing public opposition. However, several countries have reduced price subsidies without major political upheaval. After an initial failed attempt Tunisia was able to implement subsidy reform successfully by explaining the need for reform to the citizenry (box 2.1). Several other countries in the Middle East and North Africa, including Algeria, Egypt, Jordan, Morocco, and Yemen, have also been successful in reforming extensive food subsidies.[25] Several Eastern European countries have successfully replaced price subsidies on utilities by doing so gradually and replacing them in part with targeted cash subsidies to help households least able to cope.

Decentralization of public spending creates practical problems

Beginning in the 1980s in Latin America and in the 1990s in Asia, decentralization spread rapidly around the developing world as country after country attempted to decentralize public services to lower levels of government.[26] Decentralization has been driven largely by political, not budgetary or administrative, considerations. Adjustments to make it work can take many years as public management and expenditure responsibilities slowly catch up to the changes.

Decentralization results in the downsizing of central administration and bureaucracies, elimination of superfluous layers of bureaucracy, and empowerment of local governments. But a critical part of decentralization is the devolution of government expenditure, staffing, and allocation decision authority from a central administration to lower levels of government. In these areas, much remains to be done, even in countries where decentralization has proceeded swiftly.

Budgetary autonomy to local governments

Decentralization in developing countries often tends to assign responsibilities to local governments to deliver services without giving them budgetary power and autonomy to carry out the responsibilities. Many central governments are reluctant to cede

BOX 2.1
Implementing food subsidy reform in Tunisia

Until the early 1990s Tunisia had an extensive system of universal food subsidies (with nearly 80 percent of the population benefiting). The subsidies were intended to stabilize prices and protect the poor and vulnerable from high prices. However, by 1990, the cost of the food subsidies had risen sharply (largely because of extensive leakage of subsidy benefits to the better-off) to 3 percent of GDP. An initial attempt to reform food subsidies failed as public riots erupted when subsidies were removed.

Beginning in the early 1990s, Tunisia tried again. This time, food subsidies were lowered gradually so that the rise in food prices was also gradual. Subsidies were maintained on foods typically bought by the poor and not much in demand at higher income levels, while those on other foods were phased out to minimize the leakage of subsidy benefits to the better-off. The entire reform package was announced well in advance so that consumers could adapt to the price increases. And since the riots accompanying the earlier reforms had been instigated largely by students, the reform was announced in the summer months when universities were closed.

The government also launched an awareness campaign to explain why removing the subsidies was important for fiscal reform and would release funds for other social programs. In addition, the government introduced compensatory measures for vulnerable groups that were most affected by the rise in food prices. Finally, the government liberalized and developed markets in the foods preferred by the better-off (on which subsidies had been withdrawn), so that high-income households could consume more of them, leaving the still slightly subsidized, but less desired by the rich, foods for the poor.

Source: World Bank 1999; Tuck and Lindert 1996; Pearce 1999.

control over expenditure allocation decisions to local governments for fear that this will result in a loosening of spending controls and in greater corruption and misuse of resources. Thus in West Africa, for example, local government expenditures account for no more than 5 percent of central government expenditure (table 2.11).

Yet there is compelling evidence that subnational governments need some budget autonomy in order to deliver services effectively and respond to local needs.[27] They also need to be held accountable for the use of the resources. Balancing autonomy and accountability is a key challenge of budgetary decentralization.

Autonomy includes the flexibility to let local government units differentiate their expenditure policies for lower levels of government. This would allow provincial governments, for example, to adapt their policies toward districts or villages to account for intraprovincial variations and diversity, thus improving efficiency and equity in resource mobilization and allocation. There is always a risk that provincial governments might shift expenditure responsibilities, but not revenues, to lower

TABLE 2.11

Relative weight of local government budgets in selected West African countries, 1992 (percent)

Item	Benin	Burkina Faso	Cameroon	Côte d'Ivoire	Senegal
Share of GDP of central government	13	15	18	23	20
Share of GDP of local government	0.3	0.3	0.8	0.9	0.9
Local government as a share of the central government	2	2	5	4	5
Largest city (metro area)					
Share of total local expenditure	73	66	68	65	71
Share on national population	11	8	8	22	22
Second largest city					
Share on total local expenditure	10	22	17	6	3
Share on national population	4	4	7	4	3

Source: Farvacque-Vitkovi and Godin 1997; Brosio 2000.

levels of government, retaining a larger proportion of central government transfers for their own use. In addition to being inequitable, this would make it difficult for all districts and villages to effectively implement central government policies. But as long as provincial governments are held accountable for the performance of all their subprovincial units on key national goals, they will have the right incentives to allocate resources according to need and to both provide autonomy and demand accountability.

Budgetary autonomy requires that subnational governments be able to plan and approve their own budgets separately from those of the central government. It also requires that subnational governments have the flexibility to allocate expenditures across needs that are based on their own priorities and to choose the most cost-effective combination of inputs to deliver public services.[28] To further national goals, many countries place tight restrictions on how subnational governments can spend their resources. For instance, local governments have to reconcile their budgets in line-item detail and are not allowed to reallocate spending across narrow categories of expenditure without formal approval from the central ministry of finance. In other countries, local governments have to conform to strict physical and allocative norms provided by central sectoral ministries. This type of spending control stifles efficiency in input choices at the local level and prevents local governments from becoming more responsible and accountable for their expenditures.

A better approach is for the central government to provide budgetary autonomy to local governments while creating strong incentives for them to pursue national objectives. One example is a conditional matching grant: the central government matches, on a one-for-one or even two-for-one basis, expenditures by subnational governments on items of national importance.[29] This mechanism will not be as effective as a central government grant conditioned on attainment of specific social outcomes, but it will encourage local governments to allocate more funds to national-priority activities than they might otherwise have. A shortcoming of matching grants is that they can lead to greater inequities because wealthier local governments are better able to afford matching contributions. The central government can address this problem through alternative policy mechanisms, such as equalizing grants.

Vietnam has gone from a highly centralized to a highly decentralized economy over the last decade. With passage of the 1996 State Budget Law, the central government began devolving many government functions to subnational governments. The share of subnational governments in total public expenditure rose from 26 percent in 1992 to 43 percent in 1998 to 48 percent in 2002.[30] In 1999 the central government piloted an experiment in the province of Ho Chi Minh City to introduce block grants or lump sum budgeting, along with more flexible personnel arrangements (box 2.2). In 2002 the State Budget Law substantially increased the authority of provincial governments to organize the budgets of their district and commune governments and conferred additional recurrent budget flexibility on all levels of government. Local governments were given discretion in reallocating recurrent spending within three broad blocks of controlled expenditure—personnel expenditures, operations and maintenance, and other expenditures.[31]

Accountability of local governments

A recurring theme of public expenditure reviews is that increased accountability must accompany greater budgetary autonomy for local governments. The accountability needs to flow sideways and down as well as up. One way to strengthen accountability is to require all subnational governments to open up proposed and executed budgets to public scrutiny, by publishing budgets in newspapers or on the Internet. Future central government grants to local governments could be made contingent on meeting the full public scrutiny requirement.[32] Increased public scrutiny is the best way of ensuring that local governments are responsive to the needs and demands of their residents—the main advantage of decentralized governance over centralized authority.

Several countries introduced greater transparency in local government budgets. For instance, Vietnam's 2002 State Budget Law requires that the final accounts for executed budgets at all levels of government be made public. The law also confers

BOX 2.2
The Ho Chi Minh City experiment

Vietnam began its decentralization reforms in 1999 with a pilot experiment in the province of Ho Chi Minh City to introduce block grant budgeting, along with more flexible personnel arrangements, in 10 districts and departments. Under the 1996 State Budget Law, spending units (subnational governments and front-line service providers) were required to receive budget approval from the Ministry of Finance at a line-item level, and they were then not allowed to reallocate spending across the nine blocks of controlled expenditure without formal approval. Spending units also had to comply with physical and allocative norms established by sectoral ministries. The objectives of the pilot were to restructure administrative units and streamline administrative procedures, rationalize administrative costs, reduce overstaffing, raise salaries by using savings from these measures, and increase transparency.

Budget appropriations to the 10 administrative units were converted into block grants with amounts fixed for three years. Within these fixed budget constraints, administrative units could reallocate expenditure between line items without having to seek permission. Administrative units were free to reduce staff numbers and to reprioritize between categories of administrative expenditures (with a few exceptions), but they had to maintain specified levels and standards of service. Any savings could be retained and used to increase staff salaries or bonuses. The direct link between cost reductions and pay increases provided a powerful incentive to do both.

Financial impacts were felt quickly. All administrative units reported large reductions in expenditures on administrative items (such as communication expenses, utility bills, routine repairs and maintenance, and purchases of goods and services), with reported financial savings in the first year of 13–29 percent. Nearly all administrative units reduced their staff numbers by about 15 percent below the staff quota, with some making bigger cuts.

Although evidence remains limited, service quality does not appear to have declined. Official administrative data show that indicators of service standards, such as waiting times, generally improved. However, there is evidence that some of the savings in the pilot units may have reflected deferral rather than elimination of expenditures. Almost all pilot units reported sizable reductions in expenditure on routine repairs and maintenance (although major repairs were not included in the block grant).

Source: World Bank 2005g.

authority on the State Audit of Vietnam to conduct external audits on the revenues and expenditures of all national and subnational governments and report the results to the National Assembly. Despite these legal requirements, public availability of budgets of local governments below the provincial level (district and commune budgets) is spotty, and the data are often incorrect. Local residents are just beginning to participate in provincial, district, and commune budget processes.[33]

Ecuador's central government has been working to improve the flow of budgetary information among levels of government since 2003. Nevertheless, reporting on local budgets remains poor. Although executed municipal and provincial budgets must be submitted to the central Ministry of Economy and Finance before the end of March each year, many local administrations still send incomplete information or completely disregard the rule.[34]

Decentralization and regional disparities

While decentralized public spending is generally desirable, too much devolution of expenditure responsibilities without a concomitant increase in revenue transfers to local governments can exacerbate regional inequalities. Consider China, which is highly decentralized. Subnational governments account for 64 percent of public spending, with counties, prefectures, and townships accounting for 43 percent of that and provincial governments for the rest.[35]

In many Chinese provinces, county and township governments are responsible for two-thirds to three-quarters of budgetary expenditures on education and health and 100 percent of expenditures for unemployment insurance and social security and welfare. Yet these lowest levels of government often do not have the resources to finance their expenditure assignments because the tax-sharing system in China has recentralized revenue assignments, depriving the lower levels of government of an important source of income, and the volume of intergovernmental transfers has not offset the fiscal imbalance at the lowest levels of government.[36]

The resulting fiscal strain has caused many counties, prefectures, and townships to shift responsibility for social expenditures down to households or to default on service provision. Since there is no centrally sponsored system of ensuring a minimum level of service provision, the poorest subprovincial governments often provide only the barest of public services. Interregional disparities in health and education services and interhousehold inequalities in social outcomes have worsened in recent years.

Budget execution and the expenditure framework are weak

Budget execution is the stage of the budget process when broad sectoral expenditure allocations are broken down into more specific allocations for programs, government agencies, and local governments. Resources get transferred to agencies and local governments for the delivery of public goods and services. Many problems beset the budget execution stage, including weak budget consolidation, separate budgeting of recurrent and capital expenditures, arrears, and unpredictable expenditures. Weak budget execution results in leakages—the siphoning off of funds intended for front-line service providers such as schools and health clinics.

Off-budget financing and budget consolidation

In the interests of transparency government budgets need to be complete and to reflect all outlays by all public agencies. It is not uncommon, however, to find considerable off-budget financing, especially of losses and contingent liabilities accumulated by state-owned enterprises, some military spending, and indirect subsidies in many transition economies and in some Latin American countries. Such activities are usually financed through supplemental spending bills that bypass the normal appropriations process. Off-budgeting is most prevalent in transition economies, although it occurs in many other countries as well. Even in as advanced an economy as the United States, Congress has funded a nontrivial portion of the Iraq war by passing supplemental spending bills that circumvent the normal budget process.[37]

During President Suharto's rule in Indonesia, a significant portion of revenues from natural resources sales were diverted for government spending outside the central budget. This was possible because sales from oil and timber had minimal public visibility and could easily be hidden. President Suharto allegedly used this off-budget financing to consolidate his political power and to prevent the political conflict that would result had natural resource–rich provinces discovered that their wealth was being used to finance development programs in politically well connected states.[38] Off-budget financing had a high cost, leading to mismanagement in the oil sector, unsustainable forestry policies, and environmental degradation.

A second source of off-budget financing is bond issues (typically for infrastructure and education) by central and local governments. Expenditures from these bond revenues are typically not included in the regular budget. This practice is common in China, where subnational governments are prohibited from borrowing from nongovernmental sources on their own credit.[39] To get around this restriction, these governments create economic entities that sell "corporate" bonds, whose proceeds are used to finance infrastructure and other investments.[40]

A third source of off-budget financing is user fees, especially at service facilities like health clinics and schools. To the extent that these fees are retained at the local level—by either the facility or local governments—any expenditure out of user fees is typically not reflected in the regular public budget. In Kenya, for instance, secondary schools spend heavily out of their own revenues, spending that is typically not included in expenditures reported by the Ministry of Education.[41] User fees need to be included in expenditure planning to give governments and education ministries a complete picture of the full costs of secondary education. Reporting of user fee income, even when fees are retained by the school, would increase transparency and accountability for those funds and provide information needed by the central government to offset lower user fee collections in poorer communities.

Finally, donor financing also contributes to incomplete budget coverage. Despite recent efforts at coordination, most donors have their own disbursement mechanisms that are independent of the government. It is not unusual for the same donor to have separate disbursement mechanisms for each of its projects in a country. Much donor assistance is disbursed by project management units, which deal with the concerned line ministry and frequently do not inform the ministry of finance about disbursements. Some donor projects are executed entirely by donors. Information on grants directly executed by donors is fragmented across government ministries and departments and not available centrally. This lack of information on donor projects hampers the ability to plan and coordinate total resource allocations within the economy.

This is especially problematic in African countries, where foreign aid is large relative to GDP and accounts for a large share of public expenditure (box 2.3). In Zambia, for instance, the ratio of public expenditure financed by foreign grants to that financed by domestic revenue was as much as one-half in 1999 and one-third in 2000.[42] While estimates of donor financing are incorporated in the Zambian government budget, most aid-financed projects are executed outside of the line ministries, either directly by donors or by nongovernmental organizations on behalf of donors. Consequently, actual donor disbursements and expenditure are not systematically verified, consolidated, and accounted for.

Afghanistan is another aid-dependent country in which a significant share of foreign aid circumvents the government budget. Government estimates suggest that only 10–20 percent of donor financing flowed through the government's systems in 2002–04.[43] In 2007, Afghanistan's ambassador to the United States, H.E. Said Jawad, stated that "only 5 percent [of financial assistance given to Afghanistan] has been given to the Afghan government. Twelve percent of the funds have been given to the Afghan reconstruction trust fund. . . . The remaining 82 or 83 percent . . . has been spent outside the budget and control of the Afghan government."[44]

The off-budget share can be considerable. For instance, in Armenia off-budget expenditures—funded by noncash external grants, sectoral extrabudgetary funds, and quasi-fiscal subsidies held by state-owned energy enterprises—constituted an estimated 5–6 percent of GDP in 2000.[45] Fully consolidated, public spending amounted to 30 percent of GDP (not the 24–25 percent reported in the government budget). In some ministries, such as the Ministry of State Revenues, extrabudgetary

BOX 2.3
Aid dependence in Africa

Aid dependence is widespread in Africa. Data from *World Development Report 2008* show that 10 countries in Africa receive $50 or more in official development assistance per capita, with some countries (Eritrea and Zambia) receiving as much as $81 per capita (see table). Thus, aid constitutes as much as one-fifth to one-half of GDP—and between two to four times gross capital formation—in the poorest African countries.

Official development assistance in selected African countries, 2005

Country	Per capita ($)	Share of GDP (percent)	Share of gross capital formation (percent)
Angola	28	1.4	17.7
Benin	41	7.6	38.0
Burkina Faso	50	10.9	—
Burundi	48	48.0	400.0
Central African Republic	24	6.7	—
Chad	39	8.1	36.9
Eritrea	81	40.5	213.2
Ghana	51	9.8	30.6
Guinea	20	4.9	37.5
Kenya	22	3.8	22.3
Madagascar	50	17.9	71.4
Malawi	45	26.5	165.4
Mali	51	11.6	48.3
Mauritania	62	8.4	36.4
Mozambique	65	19.1	76.5
Rwanda	64	25.6	121.9
Sierra Leone	62	25.8	172.2
Tanzania	39	11.1	58.6
Uganda	42	14.0	56.0
Zambia	81	12.9	47.6

— is not available.
Source: World Bank 2007d.

funds accounted for 60 percent of the regular budget.[46] The Organisation for Economic Co-operation and Development estimates that China's officially reported spending accounts for only about three-quarters of total government spending, with extrabudgetary spending accounting for the rest.[47] In Nigeria about a third of total federal government expenditures remained off budget in 2005. The main types of off-budget spending included oil sector investments, some external debt service, other priority development projects funded from excess oil revenues, and statutory extrabudgetary funds.[48]

Most countries in Latin America use some off-budget accounts. For instance, Chile does not include its Ministry of Defense and its national copper company in its budget and accounting systems, and some copper company profits are transferred directly to the Ministry of Defense to provide independent funding for the military. However, both the Ministry of Defense and the copper company report their results on a net basis to parliament, so very little of the operations of Chile's central government escapes scrutiny.[49] Argentina had few off-budget accounts in 2001, before the most recent crisis. At the height of the crisis in 2002 the government created some off-budget accounts to protect favored programs from the broad cuts being imposed on the budget. Since then, although the country has largely recovered from the crisis, the number of off-budget activities has increased.[50]

There is little justification for excluding public activities and expenditures from the public budget and not subjecting them to a vote in the legislature. Such budget fragmentation makes it more difficult for public watchdogs to know how the government is spending resources and to demand accountability.

Expanding budget coverage to include all user fees and contributions and all government debt, including on-lending and off-budget bonds, should be a high priority of public expenditure reform. Budgets need to include estimates of guaranteed debts and other government contingent liabilities. And donors need to be encouraged to report and channel all their aid through the treasury. Off-budget donor spending, especially in aid-dependent African countries, undermines accountability and reduces the effectiveness of public spending in many ways. For example, a donor may lavishly fund an HIV treatment center in a building where the government operates a rundown primary care center. The donor maintains separate logistics operations; its personnel and supplies cannot be used in the government side of the building.

Dual budgeting

Dual budgeting—separating recurrent and capital expenditure decisions—is another common budget practice addressed by many public expenditure reviews. In many countries, separate ministries are involved in these two aspects of budget setting. The ministry of finance typically prepares the fiscal framework and the recurrent budget estimates, and another agency (such as the ministry of planning, the ministry of investment, or the planning commission) prepares the public investment program and the investment budget, including capital expenditures and donor-funded projects.[51] In India, for instance, the Constitution mandates separation of recurrent and capital expenditures. In addition, the government maintains a strict distinction between plan and nonplan expenditures. The Planning Commission determines planning expenditures (which include both capital and recurrent components), while the Ministry of Finance approves the allocation of nonplan expenditures, which are typically requested by line ministries.

Dual budgeting results in poor coordination of capital and recurrent spending. Capital investments are made without ensuring that the future recurrent needs of the project will be met. As a result, physical capital (such as roads) deteriorates prematurely as maintenance and rehabilitation are neglected (both are financed out of recurrent expenditures), more hospitals are built than can be adequately funded for drugs and medical supplies, and schools lack funding for books.

The opportunity cost of resources is the same whether they are spent on recurrent or investment items. Fragmenting the two decisions introduces inefficiency in the allocation of budget resources. One solution to dual budgeting is the medium-term expenditure framework, which introduces a multiyear perspective to annual budgeting and integrates recurrent and capital budgeting. Its preparation involves ministries responsible for recurrent and capital budgeting. By some counts, more than three dozen countries in Africa, Asia, and Latin America now employ a medium-term expenditure framework. The framework has become standard in the World Bank's public expenditure management toolkit. A medium-term expenditure framework allows for better macroeconomic balance, coordination across sectors, greater predictability in policy and funding, and increased autonomy of ministries (box 2.4).

BOX 2.4
Objectives of a medium-term expenditure framework

- Improving macroeconomic balance by developing a single, consistent, and realistic resource framework.
- Improving the allocation of resources to strategic priorities between and within sectors by building budgets around a single, consistent, and realistic set of policy objectives.
- Improving coordination and balance between capital and recurrent expenditures by integrating planning for both within a single, forward-looking budgetary process.
- Increasing commitment and predictability in policy and funding so that ministries and provinces can plan ahead and programs can be sustained.
- Providing ministries and provinces with a hard budget constraint and increased autonomy, improving incentives for efficient and effective use of funds.

Source: World Bank 2005g, table 4.1.

The government of Vietnam began piloting a medium-term expenditure frame-work in four sectors (education, health, agriculture and rural development, and transport) and four provinces in 2004. Its objective was to harmonize capital and recurrent expenditure budgeting across an entire sector within a single, forward-looking macroeconomic and expenditure framework and with a single, unified set of development goals. The government established an interministerial working group of senior officials of the Ministry of Finance and the Ministry of Planning and Investment, as well as interministerial groups within the four pilot sectors, with representatives of the finance and planning functions of the relevant sector ministry and the sectoral expenditure specialists from the Ministry of Finance and the Ministry of Planning and Investment. After the successful pilots, the medium-term expenditure framework was extended nationally.

Budget arrears

Arrears are another common problem in budget execution and management. Arrears arise because of unrealistic budget preparation that overestimates revenue and underestimates expenditure. They may also reflect a lack of commitment to adhere to a hard budget constraint. Large arrears from past fiscal years weaken the execution of the current year's budget.

Arrears are large in many developing countries. In Ecuador arrears constituted nearly a third of government expenditure in 2000—well above the international norm of 5 percent.[52] In Kenya expenditure arrears totaled approximately 2 per-cent of GDP in 2003, mainly in the form of unpaid bills for utilities, reflecting a tendency among many government departments to use appropriations allocated to utilities for other spending items.[53] In Armenia the stock of arrears as a percent-age of GDP was even higher—5.6 percent in 1999, 6.25 percent in 2000, and 5.5 percent in 2001.[54]

Large arrears almost always reflect weak financial compliance and a lack of budget discipline. The Russian Federation, for example, was able to virtually elimi-nate noncash budget execution and pension and wage arrears by 2002 through improved budget discipline.[55] Robust economic growth following the 1998 crisis contributed to the growth of budget revenues and made it easier for the govern-ment to eliminate arrears.

Budget classification

An important element of opening up budget information to public scrutiny is ensur-ing that budget classifications are easy for everyone to understand and analyze. Many countries use antiquated budget classifications that lack sufficient detail to account for transactions. Often, the use of budget coding is inconsistent across line ministries, making it difficult to compare budgets across sectors. China's budget classification system, for instance, is a holdover from the days of central planning and uses a mix of functional, economic, and organizational categories that do not distinguish clearly between investment and recurrent expenditures. Expenditures by different ministries do not represent functional categories, while a single function can sometimes be split across several headings. For example, administrative expenditures are scattered throughout several headings, including "administration" and "other administration."[56] In Kenya teacher salary costs are included under "general administration," making it difficult to meaningfully analyze the costs of service delivery.[57]

The International Monetary Fund has proposed an international standard for budget classification, the Government Finance Statistics (GFS) system. The 2001 GFS system makes it easy to analyze the functional composition of government expenditure, such as total amount spent by type of social service. Several countries, especially in Latin America, have adopted this standard (Argentina, Brazil, Colombia, Dominican Republic, El Salvador, Panama, and Uruguay). But even in these countries, few local governments report their expenditures in GFS detail.

Tanzania has benefited considerably from adopting the GFS coding system. In the late 1990s the government saw the need for a new classification system because of the weaknesses in its budget coding system, which was inconsistent with performance-based budgeting.[58] The government wanted a consistent and unified classification system that would let it determine exactly what was being spent on different services and assess the outcomes associated with the spending. Reclassification of the budget to the GFS standard began in 1999. The transition was gradual, starting with the economic classification of the recurrent budgets of ministries, departments, and regions. Next, the budgets of the local government authorities were reclassified. By 2001/02 the entire recurrent budget was processed using GFS item codes, and the development budget followed suit by 2003/04.

Adoption of the new economic classification has greatly improved the coding of budget estimates in Tanzania, helping to identify the details of expenditure allocations to education, health, water, agriculture, roads, and general activities. More important, it enabled the introduction of performance budgeting.[59] Resource allocation is now linked to specific quantitative and monitorable targets, and management accountability has been enhanced through performance monitoring and reviews.

Expenditure leakages
An important manifestation of poor budget execution is the failure of public funds to reach their intended beneficiaries. During the 1990s, Public Expenditure

Tracking Surveys were developed to track the flow of public funds through the administrative hierarchy, from the central government to the front-line service providers (health facilities, health staff, schools, and teachers).

The surveys identify not only the extent of fund leakage (the difference between the amount of funds disbursed and the amount received by service facilities) but also the amount of leakage at each step of the delivery chain and potential reasons for the leakage (such as institutional shortcomings, inefficient delivery arrangements, and corruption and embezzlement). In addition, the surveys enable policymakers to identify delays in resource transfers at each step.

One of the first Public Expenditure Tracking Surveys to be done was in Uganda for 1991–95. A sample of government primary schools was surveyed in selected districts to determine how much of nonsalary expenditures channeled to them through the local governments actually arrived at the schools. The survey indicated that most schools had received none of the monies from the capitation grant, even though the central government had almost fully released the entire amount of the grant to district governments. On average, schools received 13 percent of central government spending on the program, with local government officials and politicians capturing the rest. Further, there was large variation in grants received by different schools, with schools in better-off communities receiving more of the funds to which they were entitled than schools in poor communities. In addition, most districts lacked reliable records of disbursements to individual schools.[60]

The government launched a major publicity campaign to inform schools and communities about the capitation grants to which they were entitled. A follow-up public expenditure tracking survey in 2001 with virtually the same sample of schools found that schools had received 82 percent of the capitation grants. The reduction in leakages was significantly larger for schools that had been exposed to the Public Expenditure Tracking Survey publicity campaign: schools that were aware of the funds to which they were entitled were more likely to demand and get them.[61]

Public Expenditure Tracking Surveys have since been carried out in other sectors (particularly health) and in other countries in Africa, Asia, and Latin America, including Ghana, Nigeria, Rwanda, Tanzania, Zambia, Cambodia, Lao PDR, Pakistan, Colombia, Ecuador, and Peru. While findings vary, the surveys have shed light on the complex flow of funds from the national government through local governments and down to individual service facilities. They have identified major bottlenecks in expenditure execution and revealed systemic problems in need of reform.

Prospects for improving public financial management and procurement systems are mixed

Over the past decade, in addition to public expenditure reviews, the World Bank has undertaken country financial accountability assessments and country procurement assessment reviews at least once for each of its borrowing countries. Originally, these were internal documents to help World Bank staff determine how reliable country disbursement and procurement systems would be for project implementation. Many of these documents are now in the public domain. The OECD has supported a systematic evaluation framework for procurement that has been adopted by most country procurement assessment reviews.

These reviews also helped to document the quality of public financial management and implementation arrangements across countries. As World Bank staff came to understand these issues in a more systematic way, the information began to be used for policy dialogue on improving financial management, procurement systems, and implementation arrangements. A sample of these reviews for 2007 and 2008 for 10 Latin America and the Caribbean countries and 30 African countries was reviewed for lessons.

Generally, the reviews looked for characteristics of sound public expenditure management systems:

- Is there a clear legal and institutional framework for expenditure management? Is the budget comprehensive? Is the budget organized into programs? Are revenues reconciled with spending plans?
- Is there an adequate and open system to review the budget and set priorities?
- Is budget execution consistent with accountability, transparency, and efficient management of public funds? Do these systems meet the standards of economy, efficiency, competition, and transparency?
- Is there independent scrutiny of the government's stewardship of public resources, including internal and external audits, performance monitoring, vigorous legislative oversight, and opportunities for civil society oversight?

Of the 10 Latin American and Caribbean countries reviewed (Brazil, Chile, Colombia, Costa Rica, Dominican Republic, Guatemala, Honduras, Jamaica, Panama, and Paraguay) only Brazil and Chile were found to have made significant progress across the full set of measures, with Brazil making noticeable progress during the past decade and Chile consistently seeking to improve performance over the past two decades. Costa Rica and Panama have introduced some important reforms but still have many off-budget items and other peculiarities that limit their ability to plan for and meet commitments and to procure well. The remaining countries have problems across the board that they have been slow to address. Nevertheless, most have made progress at least in gaining control over the overall balance of revenue and expenditure.

Procurement is particularly troublesome. Even countries that have a legal procurement framework in place often leave procurement up to individual agencies, which develop their own rules and practices. Except in Chile and increasingly in Brazil, procurement is considered an administrative function, with the focus on following agency rules rather than on achieving the desired results of economy and efficiency. Often, agency-level procedural rules become so specific and costly to manage that bidding firms begin to specialize and develop ties to agencies, which erodes competitiveness and transparency. For both financial management and procurement, the focus is on controls and procedures, not on achieving results, except in Chile.

By far, the weakest elements in all these countries are audit and oversight. And especially in the social sectors, which depend on decentralized implementation, any controls and oversight quickly lose their force as distance from the capital increases.

For the 30 countries reviewed in Africa, the systems are in a different state of development, but the results are similar. Before the mid-1990s most African countries had inadequate legal frameworks for public financial management and procurement. Since the 1990s the World Bank and other donors have worked systematically with African governments to correct these problems. As in Latin America, most countries now have substantial control over their fiscal balance, a necessary condition for good budget management and a great step forward.

For procurement most African countries now have laws on the books based on the model developed by the United Nations Commission on International Trade Law. A considerable gap remains, however, between law and practice. Aligning them is likely to take many years, as countries develop the necessary institutions and skills and slowly abandon old practices.

The issues covered by the country financial accountability assessments have been formalized in the Public Expenditure and Financial Accountability program, which has 28 indicators (further decomposed into 73 detailed dimensions) for grading public financial management systems from A to D, with D being the worst grade. Norway recently scored itself, receiving a world record 17 As, 5 Bs, 4 C+s, and 2 Ds. The Ds were for lacking a comprehensive internal audit function and for having no systematic public reporting of resources for municipal-based service delivery units.

The scoring system has not been applied to Latin American countries, but there has been substantial coverage in Africa. For 31 African countries scores were far lower than Norway's. Although the details are complex, the core findings are consistent with the country procurement assessment reviews and country financial accountability assessments:

- Budget preparation processes are stronger than execution and oversight.
- De jure is rated higher than de facto, the problem of good law but poor implementation.
- Processes are stronger in more homogeneous environments with few actors, such as the budget department or treasury. They are much weaker where more actors or more layers are involved, such as in the decentralized operations in the social sectors.

What remains to be done

Although the focus in this chapter has been on problems, it should be acknowledged that public expenditure management in low- and middle-income countries has made considerable progress over the last two decades. Several countries have adopted comprehensive budget legislation, reduced waste and inefficiency in public expenditure, given local governments greater budget autonomy, and attempted to open budgets to public scrutiny. Nearly 40 countries around the world, led by those in Africa, have adopted the medium-term expenditure framework to guide budget formulation and execution. The framework has allowed them to introduce a multiyear perspective in annual budgets and to coordinate budgeting across sectors and functions. Scores of countries now use the Public Expenditure and Financial Accountability program, which provides consistent information for monitoring and evaluating performance. And the use of the *Government Finance Statistics Manual 2001* international standard for budget classification has improved the coding of budget estimates in many countries and helped identify the details of expenditure allocations to education, health, water, agriculture, roads, and general activities. This in turn has enabled the introduction of performance budgeting in several countries.

Yet the picture is not as bright for the feasibility of preventing or controlling corruption and improving budget execution. First, systematic knowledge and data on the performance of government systems are recent. The Public Expenditure and Financial Accountability program and the OECD's procurement frameworks are new, and implementation is even newer. The International Budget Program's Open Budget Index, which measures many of the same phenomena and is discussed in chapter 3, was developed only in 2005–06.[62] These accountability systems have not reached much beyond giving governments the ability to manage overall revenues and expenditures (a tremendous achievement, but only the first stage) and are particularly weak in decentralized service delivery. Decades of patiently investing in better governance of expenditures are likely to be needed. Improved technology can have an impact, but experience in Latin America and the Caribbean suggests that new technology grafted onto dysfunctional or incomplete systems may improve efficiency, but the systems remain dysfunctional.

Second, nothing discussed in this chapter has addressed the core source of leakages in most service delivery by government: the low productivity of service delivery personnel. That is the critical issue in education and health: how to make sure that people on the supply side of the social sectors actually produce, without forgetting that other inputs are also important.

Thus, several areas remain in which both the study and practice of public expenditure management need to be improved. Budget formulation in most developing countries still remains largely an incremental and mechanistic exercise, with excessive attention on inputs and not enough on outputs and outcomes. A part of the problem is that policymakers do not adequately understand the complex web of relationships among project interventions, sectoral policies, public expenditure, household socioeconomic outcomes, and major development goals.

Another reason for the tenuous link between a country's strategic objectives and its level and pattern of public expenditure is the vast size of most national bureaucracies. When scores of ministries, departments, provinces, and local governments are involved in the expenditure process, a lag between a change in national priorities and the reflection of these priorities in the national budget is to be expected. This is also why it may be easier for local governments, which are leaner and presumably more nimble, to adjust their budgets in response to changing priorities than for central governments to do so.

This is where a focus on communities could make a big difference. For instance, a comparison of the unit cost of providing an identical service across several different municipalities might be extremely revealing about expenditure effectiveness, as the Center for Budget and Policy Studies in Bangalore, India, discovered (box 2.5). The study highlights the importance of competition in improving expenditure effectiveness among local governments by creating a strong incentive to improve the cost effectiveness of public spending.[63]

Improving expenditure effectiveness at the local level is vitally important, as problems of budget execution, elite capture, and misuse of funds are particularly egregious at the local level. In most countries, the national budget is already under considerable scrutiny—from citizens, civil society organizations, bilateral donors, and multilateral organizations (such as the International Monetary Fund and the World Bank). However, local governments, because of their large numbers and

BOX 2.5

Comparing infrastructure services across 10 municipalities in Karnataka, India

Over 1998–2001 the Center for Budget and Policy Studies (CBPS) studied detailed budget documents and other information on the level of infrastructure created and maintained (such as number of street lamps, number of borewells, kilometers of roads, and tons of solid waste handled) for 12 urban municipalities in the state of Karnataka. The CBPS used these data to calculate the unit cost of providing and maintaining different types of infrastructure services across municipal councils and found large variations. For instance, the cost of installing and maintaining a city street lamp varied by a factor of more than 10 from one municipality to another. The study findings were an eye-opener for council members in some of the municipalities, as they learned for the first time that their municipality was paying considerably more for street lamps than a neighboring municipality. Although a follow-up survey was not done, publication of the CBPS findings likely led to reductions in disparities in unit costs across municipalities.

Source: Rao and Rath 2005; see in particular table 13 (p. 20).

geographic dispersion, are often not subject to the same attention, so there are greater opportunities to misuse public funds or to use them less effectively.

There is thus a strong need for public expenditure reviews at the subnational level. Very few World Bank public expenditure reviews have been done at the provincial or subprovincial level.[64] It is unrealistic to expect a multilateral organization such as the World Bank to undertake the thousands of subnational reviews that would be required. Nor is it clear that a centralized organization would have the community-specific knowledge and resources required to conduct effective subnational public expenditure reviews. This is a job well suited to grass-roots-based civil society organizations composed of local citizens, community workers, social activists, and teachers, assisted by professional accountants or researchers familiar with budget issues. Research support could be provided by budget research groups that already have a presence in most countries—organizations such as Unnayan Shamannay in Bangladesh, the Center for Policy Analysis in Ghana, the Center for Budget and Policy Studies in India, and Centro de Investigación de la Universidad del Pacífico in Peru.

An analogy can be drawn to the national human development reports pioneered by the United Nations Development Programme in 1990.[65] The human development report is a review of the state of human development—measured primarily by health, education, and income outcomes—across countries. Beginning in 1992, the United Nations Development Programme began promoting national human development reports, with preparation delegated to government and civil society organizations in individual countries.[66] Subsequently, many countries began undertaking subnational (state- or province-level) human development reports, which became useful planning tools to inform policy dialogue and shape human development policies.[67] More recently, a few countries have begun preparing district-level human development reports, with heavy civil society involvement.[68] More than 420 national and subnational human development reports have been produced.

Another often overlooked issue in the public expenditure reviews is the state of budget literacy. In most low- and middle-income countries there is widespread ignorance of budget and public expenditure issues among ordinary citizens, grassroots organizations, journalists, and legislators. This makes it difficult for legislators to ask the right questions of government bureaucrats and treasury officials about public spending or for journalists to probe misuse of public funds. It is also difficult to engage citizens over public expenditure mismanagement.

Notes

1. Fleshman 2002.
2. Pradhan 1996.
3. De Renzio 2005.
4. Folscher and Cole 2006.
5. Folscher and Cole 2006.
6. Pradhan 1996.
7. World Bank 2004c.
8. World Bank 2001.
9. World Bank 2005b.
10. Psacharopoulos and Patrinos 2002. Most of the estimated returns in the literature are based on cross-sectional data and do not necessarily reflect the causal effect of schooling on wages. In addition, these estimates typically do not control for unobserved heterogeneity, such as innate ability or family background, that may result in bias. A review by Card (2001) suggests that the failure to control for unobserved heterogeneity typically results in overestimating returns to schooling, while the failure to account for the endogeneity of schooling decisions causes underestimating of returns.
11. World Bank 1993.
12. World Bank 2002a.
13. World Bank 2005b.
14. Of course, it is not clear what mix of services the two hospitals provide. It is possible that tertiary-level institutions and provincial and district hospitals may be delivering a

substantial share of basic health care and primary services owing to a failure of lower level facilities and individuals bypassing these facilities.

15. World Bank 2003b.

16. World Bank 2002b.

17. UNESCO 2006.

18. UNESCO 2003.

19. World Bank 2003b.

20. World Bank 2005c.

21. World Bank 2005c.

22. In addition to economic distortions, enormous waste is often associated with these subsidies. For instance, many countries experience high losses in the power sector due to outright theft of power, incorrect billing, and transmission leakages.

23. World Bank 2004a.

24. World Bank 2002b.

25. World Bank 1999.

26. During the 1980s, for example, many Latin American countries decentralized the administration and delivery of education and health services as a logical response to political democratization. In India, decentralization began in earnest with the passage of the Local Government Act of 1992, which gave control to elected village and urban councils (panchayat raj institutions) over a wide range of government social and development activities, including education, health care, nutrition, and safe drinking water and sanitation. Likewise, greater fiscal decentralization was mandated in the Philippines by the Local Government Code of 1991 and facilitated in Vietnam by the State Budget Laws of 1996 and 2002. In the early 1990s nearly all of the countries of the former Soviet Union implemented some type of decentralization to reduce the power of the central control systems they had inherited.

27. Ahmad and others 2005; Besley and others 2004.

28. Andrews and Shah 2003.

29. Shah 2006.

30. World Bank 2005e. This ratio still remains lower than in countries like China, where subnational governments account for nearly two-thirds of total public expenditure (World Bank 2002b). But the change in China has been much slower; for instance, the subnational government share was as high as 54 percent as far back as 1978.

31. World Bank 2005e.

32. Khemani 2006.

33. World Bank 2005e.

34. World Bank 2004a.

35. World Bank 2002b.

36. World Bank 2002b.
37. Lee, Johnson, and Joyce 2007.
38. Ascher 1998.
39. Mountfield and Wong 2005.
40. Freire and Petersen 2004.
41. World Bank 2005b.
42. World Bank 2001.
43. Rubin, Hamidzada, and Stoddard 2003.
44. Said Jawad, interviewed by Robert McMahon for the Council on Foreign Relations, February 28, 2007 (www.cfr.org/publication/12739/afghanistan_lacks_capacity_to_govern.html).
45. World Bank. 2003b.
46. World Bank. 2003b.
47. OECD 2006.
48. World Bank 2007c.
49. World Bank 2005b.
50. World Bank 2003a.
51. Stevens 2004.
52. World Bank 2004a. However, the ratio of arrears to expenditure declined in subsequent years—to 15 percent in 2001 and 2002 and to 5 percent in 2003.
53. World Bank 2005b.
54. World Bank 2003b.
55. World Bank 2005e.
56. World Bank 2002b.
57. World Bank 2005b.
58. World Bank 2006b; IMF 2004; UNCDF 2006.
59. UNCDF 2006. World Bank 2005f.
60. Ablo and Reinikka 1998; Reinikka and Svensson 2000.
61. Reinikka and Svensson 2000.
62. IBP/OBI 2009.
63. In principle, it is possible to improve public expenditure effectiveness across countries in the same way. However, country comparisons of public expenditure effectiveness are significantly more complicated because of large differences in culture, history, context, and social conditions.
64. To date, the World Bank has conducted provincial public expenditure reviews in very few countries—China, India, Pakistan, and Vietnam—and even in these countries, public expenditure reviews have been done for only a few provinces and states.
65. UNDP 1990.

66. Bangladesh and Cameroon prepared the first national human development reports in 1992, followed by Botswana (1993), the Philippines (1994), and Egypt (1994).

67. One of the first subnational human development reports was the one prepared by the state of Madhya Pradesh, India, in 1995. Since then, 16 states in India have regularly produced their own human development reports. Several countries in Africa, Asia, and Latin America also produce their own subnational human development reports.

68. For instance, seven states in India now produce district-level human development reports.

The political dimension of public accountability

Chapter 2 provided a diagnosis of public expenditure and financial management in developing countries, identifying progress and challenges. Despite substantial investment of time and resources by the international community to support improvements in budget management, public expenditure and financial management in many developing countries remains generally disappointing, especially at the subnational level.

This is not surprising. Securing public accountability is not only a technical challenge, but also a political one. In a political system with no effective demand for transparency and accountability, efforts to promote improved techniques are unlikely to succeed. But in systems where there is demand for improved transparency and accountability, new tools can help translate demand into results. Effective demand alone does not guarantee high standards of transparency and accountability, however; also crucial are strong institutions and appropriate tools.

Defining the problem

Before exploring the political dimensions of accountability, it is helpful to identify the types of governance problems encountered in public financial management. The root causes of system deficiencies can be broadly categorized as corruption, inefficiency, and bad policy choices. Each requires a different set of interventions for improving the system and the outcomes.

Corruption has emerged from the shadows as a critical issue for development. Led by groups like Transparency International, the campaign against corruption has raised awareness of the extent of the problem. Corruption is no longer excused as part of the local culture. But while awareness of the case against corruption has grown, rooting it out continues to be difficult, with progress coming one agency and one country at a time.

Inefficiency, though less likely to attract the attention of international campaigners than corruption is, may account for greater losses of public resources. Because inefficiency is often the result of unqualified staff performing functions beyond their capacity, one solution is enhanced training for officials responsible for budget formulation and implementation.

The final root cause of questionable public financial management—deliberate policy choices—is more problematic. How a government allocates its budget is a sovereign political decision. While international norms and standards are often applied, how much money should be spent and in which sectors depends on each country's needs and wants. Thus, translating diagnosis into action on problems involving policy priorities is tricky, best dealt with through home-grown, domestic accountability mechanisms.

Whatever the origin and nature of the problems, demand for change and the incentives it creates are key to improving public financial management systems and public expenditure outcomes. On corruption and inefficiency the international community has already taken a strong lead, and domestic organizations in many developing countries have taken up the cause with vigor, promoting transparency and minimum standards for public officials. But the international community has less influence over misguided policy decisions. While it can advise against them, that is seldom adequate. Needed is a domestic groundswell that compels governments to listen to its citizens' demands about public expenditure outlays and social policy decisions. The remainder of this chapter presents a framework for how such citizen action could be generated and channeled to best effect.

Applying the principal-agent framework to citizens seeking results from government

As argued in chapter 1, achieving public accountability is ultimately a political challenge. There are different routes to accountability. This section develops the principal-agent relationship model as a framework for discussing alternative systems of accountability.

The classic example of the principal-agent relationship is that of a professional manager (agent) hired to run a firm on behalf of the owner (principal). Problems can develop in the relationship if the agent's interests differ substantially from the principal's and if the principal cannot easily observe the agent's performance and compel the agent to behave in accordance with the principal's interests.[1]

By extension, the principal-agent model has been used to explore the relationship between government and the public.[2] The model begins with the premise that a government's legitimacy and authority derive from the consent of those it governs. In a democracy there is an understanding that the primary purpose of government is to serve the interests of the electorate. But even in nondemocratic systems it is analytically useful to view the government (as well as specific government units or individual officials) as agents and the general public as principals and to ask how well the public is able to influence the actions of the agent.

Certain aspects of the relationship are fundamental to the principal's efforts to hold the agent accountable. These include selecting the agent, designing the policy and institutional environment in which the agent operates, observing the agent's behavior, and responding to any identified problems.

Selecting the agent

Selecting the agent is a key step in the principal-agent relationship. It matters what methods are used for selecting—and, crucially, for dismissing—agents. These methods are an important part of the incentive framework in which agents operate. Effective methods for choosing an agent increase the likelihood that agents will represent the principal's interests and provide mechanisms for removing agents who have been unresponsive or ineffective.

In the context of public spending and service delivery, agent selection occurs at multiple levels, with the nature of the agent and the selection processes subject to the structure of the government (table 3.1). Of the various selection methods, only in elections does the principal (the public) do the selecting directly. With the other methods, the agent is generally selected by a higher level agent.

Designing the policy and institutional environment

Government entities work within policy and institutional environments that set the entities' responsibilities, the processes within which the entities operate, the resources and support that will enable the entities to complete their duties, and the incentives and the controls to ensure that entities function honestly and efficiently. The institutional environment also includes the culture within which the agent operates. A well designed policy and institutional environment can increase accountability, though strong rules alone are rarely adequate to ensure good performance. Table 3.2 lists the main types of agents involved in public expenditure management and some of the key policy and institutional features that affect their performance as agents.

TABLE 3.1

Agent selection methods for public expenditure functions

Functional level	Typical agents	Selection methods
Formulation	Top executive figures	Elections
	Senior bureaucrats	Political appointments or civil service hiring
	Parliamentarians	Elections
Spending/ allocation decisions	Senior executive officers	Cabinet appointments
	Senior bureaucrats	Political appointments or civil service hiring
	Subnational government officials	Local elections (or appointment)
Implementation/ execution	Bureaucrats	Civil service hiring
	Public service providers (teachers, doctors)	Bidding/contracting (for private service providers)
	Private sector partners	Procurement

Source: Authors' analysis.

TABLE 3.2

Policy and institutional features affecting public expenditure management agents

Agent	Key policy and institutional features
High-level executive officials and parliamentarians	• Checks and balance on legislative and executive powers
	• Budgeting powers and processes
	• Budgeting framework
	• Role of parliament
	• Disclosure requirements (what, when and where)
	• Participation and consultation requirements
	• Performance measurement systems (high level)
	• Accounting, reporting, and auditing processes (high level)
Senior bureaucrats and administrators	• Decentralization processes and structures
	• Rules for administrative discretion in shifting allocations
	• Accounting, reporting, and auditing processes (mid-level)
Service providers	• Amount of resources provided to support work (including reliability of resource delivery)
	• Quality of training
	• Design of compensation system
	• Accounting, reporting, and auditing requirements (service delivery level)

Source: Authors' analysis.

Enforcing accountability

The third component of the principal-agent framework for public entities is the means by which the principal holds the agent accountable for its behavior. This includes efforts made to observe the agent's behavior, as well as responses to those observations. These are discussed in the following section.

Charting the sources of accountability

Efforts to observe an agent's behavior can take several forms. The conceptual framework presented here distinguishes four broad types of accountability—top-down, sideways, bottom-up, and external (figure 3.1).

Top-down accountability

Accountability can come from higher levels of governments. This is typically the case in a centralized hierarchical system, where power flows from the top to the bottom. But not all higher level government entities are committed to enforcing accountability for the effectiveness of resource use at lower levels of government or by service providers. This lack of motivation may reflect incentives for allowing the

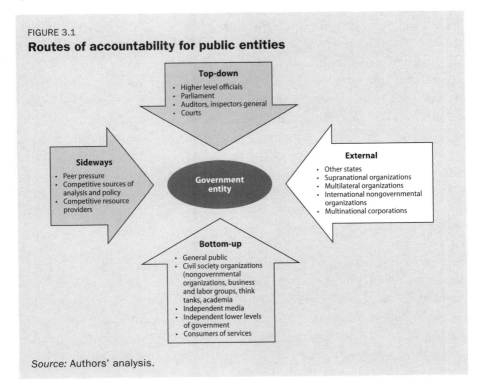

FIGURE 3.1
Routes of accountability for public entities

Top-down
- Higher level officials
- Parliament
- Auditors, inspectors general
- Courts

Sideways
- Peer pressure
- Competitive sources of analysis and policy
- Competitive resource providers

Government entity

External
- Other states
- Supranational organizations
- Multilateral organizations
- International nongovernmental organizations
- Multinational corporations

Bottom-up
- General public
- Civil society organizations (nongovernmental organizations, business and labor groups, think tanks, academia
- Independent media
- Independent lower levels of government
- Consumers of services

Source: Authors' analysis.

misuse of public resources (for example, because the abuser is part of a larger system of patronage that helps the government maintain power) or inadequate incentives for using the resources more effectively (little threat of political repercussions or no reward for improving performance). Further, even when government entities support more effective resource use, they may lack the capacity to observe the behavior of lower levels of government or to compel better behavior.

It is important to understand the conditions and forces that can encourage and enable top-down accountability. The bottom-up, sideways, and external pressures discussed below can push top-down actors to hold lower levels of government accountable. And governments, collectively or individually, may have their own interests in making improvements and can exercise their powers to improve performance. Of special importance are government units that can function as internal accountability mechanisms, which includes such entities as parliaments, courts, auditors, and inspectors general that can have express or implied top-down accountability functions.

Sideways accountability

Sideways accountability or peer pressure can be particularly effective among professional service providers. Academia provides a clear example of sideways accountability. Many university professors operate with little or no top-down (administrator) or bottom-up (student) control. Rather, their main source of accountability is to other academics or to their peers. How much of this type of peer pressure exists, or could be enhanced, among public officials is less clear. Higher skilled professionals with specialized knowledge, such as accountants and physicians, are more likely to be subject to peer pressure than are less specialized civil servants. For example, one suggestion for improving procurement is to professionalize it, as has occurred with accounting.[3] In environments with vigorous civil society organizations and active, well informed think tanks, it may be possible to apply significant peer pressure on mid- and upper-level bureaucrats as the policy process becomes more professionalized and knowledge based.

Bottom-up accountability

The ultimate source of government accountability is the public as a whole. In an ideal system, the people are able to hold their government accountable because they can monitor the government's performance and address identified shortcomings. In practice, there are many challenges to effective bottom-up accountability, particularly in developing countries. Perhaps the greatest is the collective action problem, which makes it difficult for the public to act as a group.

The collective action problem arises when members of the public have an interest in improving the quality of government performance, but the cost to any single individual of acting (whether to monitor and hold the agent accountable or to organize a collective effort to do so) would be very high and likely to outweigh any private benefits. As a result, direct action by the public will not generally occur outside of exceptional circumstances. In contrast, cohesive special interest groups, which stand to derive private benefits from acting in a specific situation (such as government subsidies) will typically be far more active in monitoring public servants than will the general public.

One way that segments of the general public can overcome the collective action problem to enforce their interests is through certain civil society organizations—such as community groups, nongovernmental organizations, research and policy organizations, and faith-based groups. Members of a collective recognize their shared interest and the need for accountability and so form civil society organizations or provide resources to support them as their proxies. Even though many individuals will not recognize their interest in leading or supporting such an effort or will prefer to act as free riders (assuming that others will act or provide the resources to support the proxy), the proliferation of community groups and nongovernmental organizations in recent years suggests that this can be a viable method of increasing accountability (see box 3.1 on bottom-up accountability and interest group theory).

Most societies also have other sources of bottom-up accountability. These include academic entities, independent news media, private businesses, and even lower level government units with some independence from the national government.

External accountability

The three channels of accountability discussed so far operate within the country system. External actors can also sometimes play a role in monitoring government. These actors include other countries (particularly neighbors, trading partners, strategic powers, and donors), supranational organizations (such as the United Nations and the European Union), multilateral organizations (such as the International Monetary Fund and the World Bank), international nongovernmental organizations (such as Amnesty International, Greenpeace, environmental organizations, and transparency and corruptions organizations), and multinational corporations.

Before the recent global wave of democratization, these institutions were the main source of accountability for many authoritarian national governments. With a submissive populace and compliant internal mechanisms, the only checks on government actions were international standards and scrutiny. In general, countries are

BOX 3.1
Bottom-up accountability and interest group theory

The simple bottom-up concept of account-ability is complicated by the "interest group" aspects of the civil society organizations that are formed. Various theories of political science seek to explain how interest groups compete to manifest their interests through the political system. In the classic plural-ist theories, accountability is found in the design of the system: if many different groups are competing, they will challenge and negotiate with each other and no one group will dominate. Thus, to the extent that the various interests within society are rep-resented in the system, the outcome of the competition will be government policies and practices representing the common good.

By contrast, competing neopluralist and corporatist theories emphasize the disproportionate power of certain groups (business interests, large landowners). Because these interest groups can exert dominion over the system, a government policy cannot be assumed to represent the common good.

Although interest group theory chal-lenges the simplified model of civil society organizations as proxies for the interest of the general public, it is consistent with the idea that the development of such organiza-tions can result in increased accountability. Whether or not individual organizations can legitimately claim to represent the public good, civil society organizations collectively can still function as a check on the power of groups that may hold sway over the govern-ment. Strengthening organizations engaged in government monitoring can transform a country from a corporatist model, character-ized by elitism, clientelism, and patronage, to a more pluralist model. Further, under interest group theory, civil society organiza-tions can function as bottom-up sources of accountability, since the threshold for contributing to accountability is whether the organization plays a role in monitor-ing government or advocating for better performance, not whether the organization individually represents the public good.

more open to these influences the more they want to participate fully in the global economy and global organizations.

Taking advantage of the changing world political context

Much has changed in the world political context over recent years to influence the domestic landscape of developing countries and the scope for holding governments accountable to the public. Three key trends have advanced the potential of bottom-up accountability: the spread of democracy; the impact of new technology, especially in information and communications; and growing governmental decentralization.

Democratization

As discussed in chapter 1, there has been an unprecedented move toward democ-racy since the 1980s. This trend has brought with it a more general push for greater openness in society and better adherence to the rule of law. Countries in all regions are experiencing the benefits of greater freedom and openness, as democratization has improved the political and social landscape in many countries. With growing democratization, many low- and middle-income countries now have political systems and institutions that offer some space for civil society to join the political process.

Technology

In addition to becoming more open, the world has become smaller through the growth and dissemination of technological innovation. The isolation and lack of information that once characterized much of the developing world are fast vanishing. Information and communication technology is increasingly exposing people to vast amounts of information and new ideas. For decades communication links had been slow to expand because of the need for expensive infrastructure, such as cables and wires, and government monopolies that curbed their spread and permitted easy control. Now, regions of the world where landline telephones are still rare and of poor quality can have advanced and reliable cellular networks. Cellular networks are thriving even where—or maybe especially where—there is no government regulation (box 3.2).

In particular, rapid development in personal computing and the use of mobile telephones has enabled even people in the remotest areas to connect with others across the world. By the end of 2008 an estimated 3.4 billion people worldwide had at least one mobile phone, and 2.7 billion of them (75 percent) were in developing countries. The spread of access to inexpensive communications is entirely a 21st century phenomenon. In 2000 there were only 19 percent as many phones, and developing countries accounted for only 25 percent of the total. In just the 12 months to March 2009, more than 90 million new subscribers emerged in Africa alone. By 2013, 6 billion subscribers worldwide are expected, more than half of them in China and India. Mobile phone penetration (number of phones per 100 people) reached 100 percent in Europe in 2007 and is expected to reach 100 percent in Kenya and Tanzania by 2013.[4] Indeed, as discussed later, the wide availability of wireless services may substitute for Internet connectivity in poorer countries as smart phones become cheaper.

Some developing countries are leading the way in mobile technology as they embrace the communications revolution, pioneering such innovations as phone banking, enabling millions of people to access bank accounts and other products critical to economic growth. In Kenya more than 1 million customers now use the local mobile phone banking system, M-Pesa. Similar operations have emerged

BOX 3.2
Mobile success emerges amid the mayhem

Telecommunications is one of the few success stories to come out of Somalia in recent
years. The country of 8 million people has
had no functioning government since the
fall of the dictatorship of Mahammad Siad
Barre in 1991. With no regulation or taxation, and demand for a cheaper alternative
to expensive satellite communications, by
2008 Somalia had more than 12 mobile
phone operators and had reached a density
of 7.9 phones per 100 people, compared
with 40 per 100 for Africa but only 3.5 for
its neighbor Ethiopia (where mobile phones
are part of a government monopoly). In a
story seen all over Africa, mobile phones
have become crucial business tools, particularly in the large informal economy.

*Source: The Financial Times, October 4, 2006; The
Economist, September 24, 2009.*

in Bangladesh, Malaysia, the Philippines, and South Africa. Agriculture is being
transformed by inexpensive mobile phone access to information on market prices,
weather, and techniques.

Internet use has also skyrocketed in the past decade, another phenomenon that is
almost entirely of the 21st century. But even in rich countries Internet penetration, at
50–75 percent (figure 3.2), has a considerable way to go before reaching the coverage
of mobile phones. Because wireless technology is removing infrastructure and capital
constraints and promoting investments, especially in developing countries, Internet
use is likely to begin spreading much faster as a mobile phone–based technology.
Although penetration in Africa is low, at only 6.8 percent of the population, it has
increased by 1,400 percent since 2000. The spread of the Internet has intensified
demand by citizens for more and better information from their governments, initially
for commercial purposes. It has also reduced the cost to governments of providing
information. It can be only a matter of time before a high standard of disclosure
becomes not only feasible and inexpensive but also demanded by citizens worldwide.

Decentralization
Decentralization has spread rapidly around the developing world since the 1980s
as country after country attempted to decentralize public services to lower levels of government (see chapter 2). Decentralization reduces central administration
and bureaucracies, eliminates superfluous layers of bureaucracy, and empowers
local governments. Decentralization has sometimes proceeded in parallel with the
expansion of democracy.

As discussed in chapter 2, a critical part of decentralization is the devolution of government expenditure, staffing, and authority over the allocation of expenditures from a

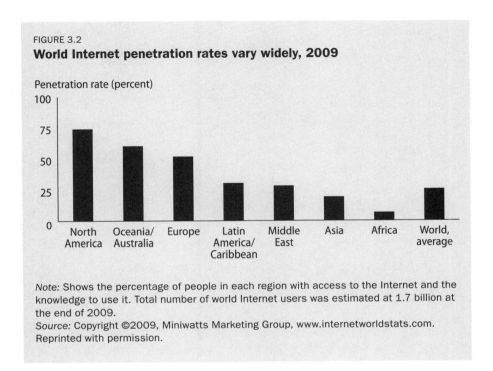

FIGURE 3.2
World Internet penetration rates vary widely, 2009

Penetration rate (percent)

Note: Shows the percentage of people in each region with access to the Internet and the knowledge to use it. Total number of world Internet users was estimated at 1.7 billion at the end of 2009.
Source: Copyright ©2009, Miniwatts Marketing Group, www.internetworldstats.com. Reprinted with permission.

central administration to lower levels of government. To deliver services effectively and responsively, subnational governments need some budget autonomy. They also need to be held accountable for the use of the resources over which they have some control. Balancing autonomy with accountability is a key challenge of budgetary decentralization.

Problems of budget execution, elite capture, and misuse of funds are particularly egregious at the local government level. Local government may be dominated by large landowners or other traditional elites, and local political life is often dominated by a single party. In small communities transactions between local government officials and contractors may be colored by long-standing personal ties. These settings may also be inhospitable to independent voices that raise unwelcome questions about the conduct of public business by the local elite, possibly making it harder to sustain a genuinely independent press or other watchdog functions.

There are reasons for concern about the quality of governance at the local level. Local governments often do not operate with the same degree of transparency in budget and expenditure decisions as the central government. In most countries central government expenditure decisions receive considerable attention from the media, public watchdog agencies, foreign donors, and international organizations. The same is not true for local governments.

Improving expenditure effectiveness at the local level is vitally important. One means of achieving greater local accountability is by requiring all subnational governments to open up proposed and executed budgets to full public scrutiny—for example, by publishing them in newspapers or on the Internet. Public expenditure reviews at the subnational level would be critical as well. Civil society organizations can help to improve transparency by creating alliances at the local level with local religious groups, local media, and political figures willing to challenge potential abuses of power. As discussed in chapter 2, decentralization creates the potential for greater accountability but by no means guarantees it. Investments in well functioning political institutions and openness to civil society involvement are essential to generate that accountability. There are many countervailing forces at work at the local level that can cripple the ability to support greater accountability.

Improving prospects for demand-driven accountability

In today's more open, more connected world there are new opportunities for using analytic tools for improving accountability and achieving better public expenditure outcomes. These tools, such as public expenditure reviews, program budget analysis,

---

BOX 3.3
Access to information laws

Access to information is a precondition for public scrutiny and a building block for greater accountability and open government. In 1980, less than a third of Organisation for Economic Co-operation and Development (OECD) countries had adopted laws guaranteeing access to information, but by 2005 nearly all (29 of 30) had. The trend has spread beyond OECD members: according to a 2006 Open Society study, 65 countries have adopted access to information laws, 53 of them within the past decade. The OECD considers these measures too new in many countries to have had an impact on government effectiveness. But they offer great potential for mutual learning.

The Czech Republic passed its Freedom of Information Act in 1999, but in practice information is still not easy to obtain. Even in the United States, which adopted its Freedom of Information Act in 1966, there has been dissatisfaction with how the law has been implemented. One-third of requests for information are rejected, and only 6 percent of requests come from the general public. Amendments adopted in 2007 added stricter deadlines, instituted a tracking system for requests, established penalties for foot-dragging, created an ombuds office to mediate disputes, and included private contractors in the scope of the legislation.

Source: Open Society 2006; Caddy, Peixoto, and McNeil 2007; SIGMA 2002; *New York Times,* "Information Con Game," December 22, 2007.

benefit (or expenditure) incidence analysis, public expenditure tracking, analysis of service delivery costs and quality, cost effectiveness analysis, and project evaluation, were previously and almost exclusively used by international organizations.

But moving these techniques into wider use by domestic policy analysts and advocates will not happen automatically. It requires opening up the state through freer access to information and increasing trust in politicians and public institutions so that analyses can have an impact on policy.

Opening up the state: the power of information

An essential requirement for improving accountability is adequate public information on the functioning of governments. Some 65 countries have adopted access to information laws (box 3.3).

BOX 3.4
International standards and accountability

Several organizations promote international standards for public sector financial statements, accounting, and auditing—functions that form the backbone of any accountability mechanism. Among them are the International Organization of Supreme Audit Institutions, the International Federation of Accountants, and the International Accounting Standards Board.

In addition, international development institutions and donors work to see that countries follow these standards. The International Monetary Fund (IMF) provides standards on the definition, classification, and accounting rules for government financial statistics for central, state, and local governments. The IMF and the World Bank divide responsibility for reporting on the observance of standards and codes in 12 areas including fiscal transparency, data dissemination, accounting, and auditing. These reports assess countries' progress in complying with international standards. Participation in these assessments, called Reports on the Observance of Standards and Codes, is voluntary, as is publication of the reports themselves.

Countries have a long way to go to improve public expenditure management. In-depth reviews by the IMF and the World Bank of public expenditure management systems in countries participating in debt relief showed that most of them did not have the necessary budgeting and financial management systems fully in place to track budget execution and monitor outcomes. The IMF and World Bank have since advocated that governments focus on 15 key public expenditure management issues, along with accompanying benchmarks. The broad areas covered are the budget comprehensiveness, classifications, projections, internal controls, reconciliation, reporting, and final auditing of accounts.

Source: IMF 2001, 2006, various years.

BOX 3.5
Trust in nongovernmental organizations among opinion leaders

Since 2001, the Edelman Trust Barometer has been measuring the level of trust among opinion leaders that various institutions will "do the right thing." These institutions include government, business, the media, nongovernmental organizations and religious groups. The results from the 2007 survey of 18 countries show that nongovernmental organizations were the most trusted of all institutions in Canada, France, Germany, Italy, Japan, the Republic of Korea (tied with business), Mexico (tied with business), Poland, Spain, and the United States. The share of survey respondents that rated nongovernmental organizations as the most trusted ranged from 60 percent in France to 29 percent in Sweden. Governments were the least trusted on average, with the share of those ranking governments the highest ranging from a low of 17 percent in Poland to a high of 78 percent in China.

Source: Edelman Trust Barometer 2007.

Establishing a legal right to public access to information about government operations is only the first step. Public agencies have an incentive to protect the considerable advantage they derive from their specific institutional knowledge on public policies and programs, rules, and regulations.[5] Ways are needed to ensure the reliability of the information that a government releases. In a survey of perceptions of public sector organizations (local hospitals, municipal councils, and police forces) in the United Kingdom, respondents complained that these institutions did not learn from their mistakes, were not always open and honest about their mistakes, and generally provided poor information about their performance.[6]

Civil society organizations can help by increasing demand for information, especially for data for measuring the quality of public spending. So can international organizations, by lobbying for access to information. They are already doing this with international standards of reporting and disclosure of public finances, but they could do much more (box 3.4).

Fixing the system will take trust

Trust is a necessary condition for independent monitoring organizations to operate effectively. Public trust in politicians and public institutions is chronically low in many countries and is waning in others.[7] For example, the latest results of Latinobarómetro's 2009 survey of public opinion found that only 24 percent of respondents put some or a lot of trust in political parties, and 45 percent in governments.[8] Trust in the judicial branch was also low, at 32 percent. The most trusted segments of society included firefighters, religious organizations, the poor, and some media.

The credibility of the armed forces has been increasing in the past 10 years—perhaps related to its withdrawal from a political role in government—while trust in the judicial branch, parliament, and political parties has remained low. However, trust in government has advanced steadily, and in 2009 it reached parity with trust in the armed forces.

These results contrast sharply with the high trust in nongovernmental organizations, putting civil society organizations in a privileged position (box 3.5). This is a niche that independent monitoring organizations can exploit: the trust that they can engender in examining and critiquing how public monies are spent may be their biggest asset. But independent monitoring organizations, like any other organization, have to earn that trust by performing to a high standard, acting consistently and predictably, communicating openly and accurately, and showing concern for results.[9] If nongovernmental organizations follow hidden agendas, they may sacrifice the trust they currently enjoy. Others who aspire to promote transparency and accountability in the public arena need to model these qualities within their own operations.

Notes

1. Eisenhardt 1989.
2. See, for example, Nyman, Nilsson, and Rapp 2005; Lane 2005; Smith and Bertozzi 1998.
3. Ladipo, Sanchez, and Sopher 2009.
4. *The Economist,* "A special report on telecoms in emerging markets," September 24, 2009.
5. Williamson 1985.
6. MORI Social Research Institute for the Audit Commission 2003.
7. The World Values Survey has been tracking trust in public institutions since the 1980s. The World Economic Forum also has carried out surveys on trust in public institutions since 2001, which show a general decline.
8. Corporacion Latinobarometro 2009.
9. Lewicki and Tomlinson 2003; Ramkumar and Krafchik 2007.

Chapter 4

Transparency and accountability in budgets and expenditure management

Chapter 2 suggests that national budgeting and expenditure management have fallen short of best practices but that the push to decentralize decisions to increase accountability to citizens could be risky under current control environments. On the positive side, chapter 3 argues that the democracy movement that has swept the world over the past two decades and the spread of cheap, more widely available information technology could transform the capability of citizens and domestic civil society institutions to hold governments more accountable for expenditure decisions and budget execution. Clearly, their role could be important not only at the central level but also at the local level, where internal accountability systems tend to work more poorly, where outsiders face enormous disadvantages in access and language, and where most spending decisions and service delivery activities that affect people's lives take place.

A necessary condition for the bottom-up and sideways pathways described in chapter 3 to function is that information about what the government is doing be freely available to citizens. This chapter addresses the question of the budget process itself and the degree to which it is open to outside scrutiny. Thomas Jefferson anticipated these concerns when he commented to Treasury Secretary Albert Gallatin:[1]

> We might hope to see the finances of the Union as clear and intelligible as a merchant's books, so that every member of Congress and every man of any mind in the Union should be able to comprehend them, to investigate abuses,

and consequently to control them. Our predecessors have endeavored by intricacies of system and shuffling the investigation over from one office to another, to cover everything from detection. I hope we shall go in the contrary direction, and that, by our honest and judicious reformation, we may be able . . . to bring things back to that simple and intelligible system on which they should have been organized at first.

Making budgets clear and transparent

What do we know about good practice in the public budget cycle? From formulating a prebudget statement months before the start of the fiscal year to evaluating the effectiveness of the previous year's budget implementation, a country's budgeting process should involve extensive consultation and documentation by stakeholders, including the executive, the legislature, and civil society. The Organisation for Economic Co-operation and Development (OECD) has created guidelines for best practices for budget transparency, including reports and documents to be created and made publicly available during each stage of the budget process (figure 4.1).[2] These stages are prioritization, execution, and evaluation of outcomes.

The prioritization stage encompasses all documents prepared and decisions made in leading up to the start of the fiscal year, including budget formulation by the executive and legislative consideration of key budget documents. At least

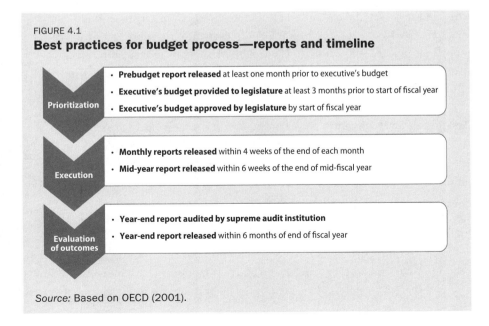

FIGURE 4.1

Best practices for budget process—reports and timeline

Prioritization
- **Prebudget report released** at least one month prior to executive's budget
- **Executive's budget provided to legislature** at least 3 months prior to start of fiscal year
- **Executive's budget approved by legislature** by start of fiscal year

Execution
- **Monthly reports released** within 4 weeks of the end of each month
- **Mid-year report released** within 6 weeks of the end of mid-fiscal year

Evaluation of outcomes
- **Year-end report audited by supreme audit institution**
- **Year-end report released** within 6 months of end of fiscal year

Source: Based on OECD (2001).

one month before the release of the draft budget (referred to in figure 4.1 as the executive's budget), the government should release a prebudget report presenting longer term economic goals and setting the stage for the more detailed executive's budget. At least three months before the start of the fiscal year the executive should present its proposed budget to the legislature, with adequate detail on expenditures and revenue streams—including budget allocations by program and administrative unit, performance indicators and targets, explanations of the previous year's performance, and forecasts for the medium term—for the legislature to make a fully informed decision. Stakeholder consultations should be completed and a final budget approved by the legislature by the start of the fiscal year.

The execution stage spans the fiscal year. Throughout budget implementation, the government should release monthly reports to the public on the budget cycle. Released within four weeks of the end of each month, these reports should present allocated and actual expenditures and revenues and should explain any adjustments to the budget. Within six weeks of the mid-point of the fiscal year, the executive should release a more detailed mid-year report that includes updated forecasts for the medium term (at least the next two fiscal years).

At the end of the fiscal year, budget data should be gathered and analyzed to evaluate the outcomes of the past year's budget. The executive should prepare a year-end report that outlines financial outcomes (predicted and actual expenditures and revenue) and performance outcomes (based on targets and indicators in the executive's budget). The supreme audit institution should audit the year-end report and release the results to the public. Although budget monitoring occurs throughout the fiscal year, the tools needed to evaluate the effectiveness and equity of public expenditures are not generally released until after the execution stage.

Analyzing performance and transparency in the budget process

As governments make budgeting decisions and release information about public expenditures to their citizens, are they following best practice as set out in these guidelines? There is no simple answer. Budgeting practices vary across and within regions. Many countries do not follow best practices guidelines, or there are extensive delays in providing budget expenditure data to legislatures, citizens, and civil society organizations. For independent monitoring organizations to formulate strategies to hold governments accountable for public expenditure practices, they need information and tools, such as prebudget reports, citizens' budgets, and mid-year and year-end reports. There are now several options for assessing the situation, all recent developments.

Public Expenditure and Financial Accountabilities

The Public Expenditure and Financial Accountability (PEFA) initiative, which collected its first data in 2005, covers all aspects of public financial management.[3] Comprising 28 indicators measuring the quality of domestic financial management and 3 measuring the quality of donor budget practices, PEFA takes the budget from macro to micro level and from inception to accounting for results.

PEFA's first set of measures focus on whether the budget is credible within the macro parameters of the economy (growth prospects, revenue available to the government, and budgetary actions appropriate to the current economic environment); whether it is comprehensive and transparent to the public; and whether it is connected to stated public policies and strategy. The second set of measures, from a micro or process standpoint, cover these questions: Is the budget predictable and under good control during execution? How well are records maintained and funds accounted for? Are auditing and performance feedback for the next budgeting cycle adequate?

Analysis of PEFA data for 57 countries[4] found two consistent patterns: countries perform better on the macro considerations than on the process indicators, and performance trails off considerably as the analysis moves from the beginning of the budget cycle to the end.[5] This pattern is consistent with the summary results of country procurement assessment reviews and country financial accountability assessments for Africa and Latin America covered in chapter 2.

Global Integrity Index

A second option is the Global Integrity Index, whose raw data and details of the reporting and verification process are freely available to the public.[6] Launched in 2004, this index covers a broad range of indicators that try to measure de jure and de facto openness of the government to its citizens, the vitality of democratic institutions, government checks and balances, protection of the rights of citizens, and anticorruption measures. It includes a section on government accountability and individual questions that cover budget institutions like the supreme audit authority. However, in 2009 it covered just 28 countries. Moreover, it does not have adequate detail on the budget process for the purposes of this book.

Open Budget Index

This chapter is based on a third option, data from the International Budget Partnership's Open Budget Initiative, whose first Open Budget Index was published in 2006. The 2006 index rated central government budget transparency in 59 countries, based on practices in 2005. A second survey, completed in 2009, covered government practices in 85 countries in 2008.[7] These two surveys provide details on transparency and budget practices across countries and regions over all stages of the budget process.

The Open Budget Index uses a survey instrument that follows the budget process from beginning to end and tracks whether the government prepares formal reports at each stage, whether the reports are shared with the public and the legislature, how much outside input is solicited and used, and how well end-of-cycle auditing and evaluation are used to formulate the next budget cycle. Because it pays attention to the timeline for inputs and the accessibility of the information to outsiders, it tries to account for document availability, clarity of content, and time available for outside scrutiny, areas that closely track good practices in public expenditure management consistent with OECD best practice (table 4.1).[8] From these questions it constructs an index and rates countries, hoping that benchmarking in this way will motivate countries to change their practices for the better.

In addition, the survey collects information on budget design and on the role of the legislature and the auditing agency in the budgeting process. This unique dataset provides an opportunity to analyze empirically how countries manage their budget processes, focusing on transparency and the ability of civil society organizations, legislatures, and audit authorities to review the budget and hold the executive accountable for its performance. The Open Budget Initiative data for 2008 are used in this chapter.

TABLE 4.1

Organisation for Economic Co-operation and Development best practices and the Open Budget Index

OECD best practices (figure 4.1)	Open Budget Index measures (figure 4.2)
Prioritization	Prebudget statement
	Budget summary
	Executive's budget proposal
	Supporting budget documents
	Citizens budget
	Enacted budget
Execution	In-year reports
	Mid-year report
Evaluation of outcomes	Year-end report
	Audit report

Source: Based on OECD (2001) and IBP/OBI (2009).

The core purpose of the Open Budget Index is its scoring of countries according to the transparency of their budget processes. In 2008 only six countries scored above 80: United Kingdom (88), South Africa (87), France (87), New Zealand (86), United States (82), and Norway (80). No high-income countries scored lower than 64 (Germany). Five countries in the full sample earned a score of 0 (Rwanda, Sudan, Democratic Republic of the Congo, Equatorial Guinea, and São Tomé and Príncipe). The overall results are disturbing. The Open Budget Index 2008 shows that:

> 68 of the 85 countries surveyed—80 percent—do not provide the public with the comprehensive, timely, and useful information people need to understand, participate in, and monitor the use of public funds. Almost 50 percent of the 85 countries studied provide minimal or no information. Thirty-two percent provide some information; only five countries provide extensive information.[9]

This chapter shows the details underlying that statement. It follows the budget cycle from beginning to end and reveals how 76 low- and middle-income countries perform, based on the data that feed into the Open Budget Index. As mentioned, although the Open Budget Index focuses on transparency, its measures are consistent with OECD best practices (see table 4.1). Additional questions within each Open Budget Index measure are related to public distribution. For example, the questionnaire asks about each budget report: Is the release date known at least one month in advance? Is advance notification of release sent to users and the media? Is the budget report released to the public on the same day as its official release to the media? Is the budget report available on the Internet free of charge? Are free print copies readily available outside the capital city and other big cities? Are reports written in more than one language? Are news conference held to discuss the release? Other elements of the questionnaire are just as extensive as PEFA reviews in ascertaining the comprehensiveness of budgets and details of budget execution.[10]

Countries exhibit great variation in budget document availability across the sample of low- and middle-income countries (figure 4.2). The OECD's best practices for budget transparency call for releasing a prebudget statement at least four months before the beginning of the fiscal year to facilitate debate on how well the budget reflects the medium- and long-term economic and fiscal goals of the government. Some 70 percent of the countries produce a prebudget statement, but only 30 percent make it available to the public. None of the South Asian countries and few of the Latin American countries in the sample release this statement.[11]

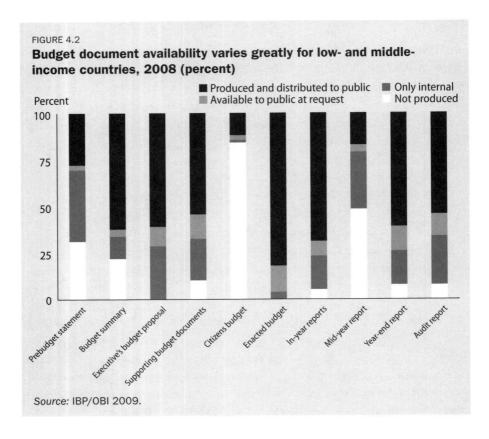

FIGURE 4.2

Budget document availability varies greatly for low- and middle-income countries, 2008 (percent)

Legend:
- Produced and distributed to public
- Only internal
- Available to public at request
- Not produced

Source: IBP/OBI 2009.

All countries in the sample produce an executive budget proposal, but only about 70 percent of them make it, the budget summary, and supporting documents available to the public. A citizens budget is a catch-all category for an effort to present the budget in a way that is easily understood by the public. It is not about receiving inputs from citizens but about taking care to report to them in an understandable way. Only 33 percent of countries (nine) in the sample do this.

The enacted budget is publicly available in more than 80 percent of the countries. In many countries this is the first budget the public sees, after the entire decisionmaking process has ended. Reporting on budget execution is not too bad, with about 70 percent of sample countries releasing these reports, but only about 50 percent produce a mid-year review of budget execution, and only 20 percent make them publicly available. Year-end reports are also produced, with about 70 percent of the countries making them available to the public. As is shown later, there are many issues surrounding these reports and their audits, and much to be learned from them for the next budget cycle.

FIGURE 4.3

Few sample low- and middle-income countries release budgets with adequate time for legislative review, 2008

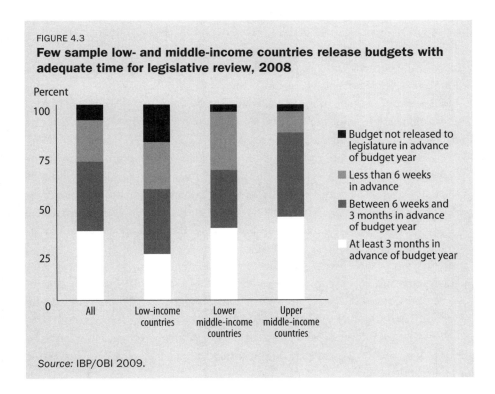

Source: IBP/OBI 2009.

The overview in figure 4.2 does not look so bad on the whole, from this bird's eye view. A handful of countries either do not produce budget reports or produce them only for the executive. This behavior is well outside accepted standards. Not producing the reports at all means that there is basically no accountability. For the 20–40 percent of countries that produce the reports and do not share them, or produce the reports and require the public to request them, there is little accountability in practice. These countries need only make access to the documents easier to substantially improve the public's ability to demand accountability, which is a core conclusion of the Open Budget Index. In most countries the reports are already produced. Transparency simply requires that they be shared with the public—the taxpayers.

The rest of the chapter delves into the details of each step in the chain summarized by figure 4.2, beginning with the prebudget statement.

Budget documents suffer from lags and incomplete data

A common problem is a late start to the budget cycle, cutting into the time for legislative oversight. The executive's budget proposals are released with varied time lags. Less than half the countries in the sample released this document at least three months before the start of the fiscal year, an OECD-recommended practice. In low-income countries this share drops to 20 percent (figure 4.3). More than 60 percent of the poorest (and aid-dependent) countries provided legislators six weeks or less to review the budget, and about 20 percent had no review.

In some countries the timing of the budget cycle results in perfunctory legislative oversight. For example, to increase legislative participation in budget formulation, Tanzania's National Assembly created sectoral budget committees in 2001 to oversee draft legislation, review budget proposals and the performance of ministries, and review audited accounts. But the parliamentary committees' oversight of the budget process began late in the budget cycle, after estimates had been prepared and approved by the Ministry of Finance and the cabinet. As a result, the ability of Parliament to question or influence sectoral allocations and ensure that they align with stated policies remained limited.

Budget proposals further complicate the oversight function by lacking adequate expenditure detail. Almost 40 percent of low- and middle-income countries surveyed presented little or no information on program-level expenditures in the budget proposal (figure 4.4). A quarter of low-income countries in the sample presented no program-level expenditures, making it difficult for legislators and the public to have an informed debate on priorities and hold the executive accountable for budget prioritization.

There is a strong connection between timely release of budget statements (see figure 4.3) and the provision of supporting material (see figure 4.4). The timely release of the budget is correlated not only with the provision of details on programs but also with a clear statement of the government's policies and priorities (0.9) and with budget grounding in a solid macroeconomic and fiscal framework (0.9). In other words, when prebudget statements are released in a timely manner, they are also accompanied by extensive supporting materials—which is necessary for budget review by the legislature and others. For budgets released with little time for review, the amount of substantiating evidence declines.

Power of the purse lies fully with the executive

Despite the importance of budgeting decisions to the public, none of the low- and middle-income countries sampled held extensive consultations with a wide range of constituencies. In most countries the executive did not consult with the public at all during budget prioritization (figure 4.5). Perhaps more surprising, in almost half of these countries the executive held no consultations with the legislature to determine budget priorities. For those that did, more than half discussed budget priorities with only a limited number of legislators. Thus, even in countries that release the budget

FIGURE 4.4

Few sample low- and middle-income countries present adequate program-level expenditures in the executive's budget proposal or supporting documents, 2008

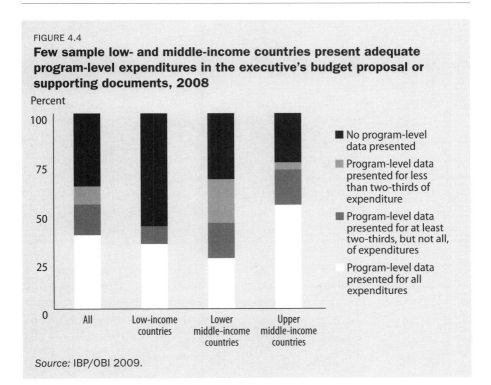

Percent

■ No program-level data presented

▨ Program-level data presented for less than two-thirds of expenditure

■ Program-level data presented for at least two-thirds, but not all, of expenditures

□ Program-level data presented for all expenditures

All | Low-income countries | Lower middle-income countries | Upper middle-income countries

Source: IBP/OBI 2009.

FIGURE 4.5

Executive consultations with key stakeholders during budget prioritization are rare in sample low- and middle-income countries, 2008

Executive consultations with the public . . .

1% — 8%
26%
65%

. . . and with the legislature

12%
7%
49%
32%

■ Holds extensive consultations with a wide range of constituencies
▨ Holds consultations with a range, but some key constituencies excluded
■ Holds limited consultations involving only a few constituencies
□ No consultations typically held

Source: IBP/OBI 2009.

proposal to the public and the legislature, the process can be flawed. Lack of consultations, timing of the budget proposal release, level of detail released, and power of the legislature to amend the proposal limit legislative and citizen oversight, even when the overall indicators on the issuing of reports may look relatively good.

Accountability is even less common than transparency. Even in countries where the budget proposal was released to the legislature and consultations were held with legislators when budget priorities were being set, many legislatures lacked the power to amend the budget proposal. Only a quarter of the low- and middle-income countries surveyed give the legislature unlimited authority to amend the budget; more than 40 percent of legislatures have minimal or no authority to amend the budget proposal (figure 4.6). Generally, the poorer the country, the more limited is the voice of the legislature in the budget process.

Involving the legislative branch and others in budget preparation does not guarantee that budgetary allocations will reflect national strategic priorities or that they will add value to the process. For example, the World Bank's public expenditure review for Indonesia notes that even though Parliament has strong powers over deliberation and approval of the annual budget, parliamentary deliberations almost always focus on "line items and discussion of details as opposed to overall allocations, political

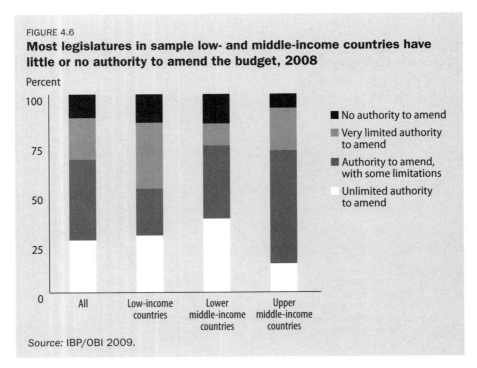

FIGURE 4.6

Most legislatures in sample low- and middle-income countries have little or no authority to amend the budget, 2008

Percent

- No authority to amend
- Very limited authority to amend
- Authority to amend, with some limitations
- Unlimited authority to amend

All | Low-income countries | Lower middle-income countries | Upper middle-income countries

Source: IBP/OBI 2009.

priorities, and achievement of results."[12] The Indonesian example suggests that an attitudinal change in thinking about budgets—and how they link to political priorities and national goals—may be the first step in budget reform in many countries. On the other hand, those who have little responsibility for the outcome may free ride on the executive and use what little power they have to pursue narrow interests or to focus on small items when the large issues are beyond their control.

Insufficient information is available to legislatures and the public during budget execution

Several problems plague budget execution and implementation. Among them are lack of budget consolidation, separate budgeting of recurrent and capital expenditures, arrears, and unpredictability in expenditures, as noted in chapter 3. Weak budget execution means that a substantial share of public expenditure does not reach front-line service providers (such as schools and health clinics).

Such shortcomings should be reviewed and documented in reports prepared during the budget implementation stage. In addition to monthly or other periodic reports the OECD suggests that countries publish a mid-year report with an updated forecast of the budget outcome for that fiscal year and a year-end report that can serve as a crucial accountability document for the government.

Both the frequency and the level of detail of periodic budget reports present obstacles to monitoring budget execution. Only a third of low- and middle-income countries sampled released monthly reports, while more than a quarter did not release any monthly reports during the fiscal year (figure 4.7). Most countries that released some reports during the year presented program-level data for all expenditures. However, a large proportion of these countries did not provide this level of detail, making it difficult for stakeholders to monitor budget implementation.

While 67 percent of countries publicly released periodic reports at least semi-annually, African countries were disproportionately less likely to release these reports. There is a poorer record of releasing a comprehensive mid-year budget report, with about 67 percent of countries not releasing it at all, failing to discuss the changes in economic outlook since the budget was enacted, or providing only limited information.[13]

The executive is nearly unaccountable to the legislature for mid-cycle budget changes

As during budget prioritization, accountability is even less prevalent than transparency in mid-cycle budget changes, indicating the weakness of important checks and balances on the executive. Half the countries did not seek legislative approval when

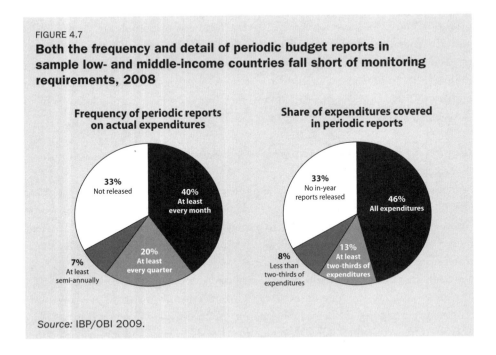

FIGURE 4.7

Both the frequency and detail of periodic budget reports in sample low- and middle-income countries fall short of monitoring requirements, 2008

Frequency of periodic reports on actual expenditures

33% Not released

40% At least every month

7% At least semi-annually

20% At least every quarter

Share of expenditures covered in periodic reports

33% No in-year reports released

46% All expenditures

8% Less than two-thirds of expenditures

13% At least two-thirds of expenditures

Source: IBP/OBI 2009.

shifting funds between administrative units during implementation (figure 4.8). In about half the low-income countries in the sample, the power to change expenditure allocations during the fiscal year lay with the executive, and the legislature had no role. In another 30 percent of low-income countries, legislative approval is sought only after the funds are shifted.

Auditing institutions are underfunded and lack independence from the executive
The independence of supreme audit institutions in conducting audits was constrained in almost a quarter of the low- and middle-income countries in the sample. Moreover, in almost half the countries, the budget of the supreme auditing institution was inadequate to fulfill its mandate (figure 4.9).

Only one in four sample low- and middle-income countries followed the OECD best practice of completing the audit of expenditures within six months of the end of the budget year (figure 4.10). Approximately 40 percent of countries either did not audit expenditures within 24 months of the end of the fiscal year or did not release audit reports to the public. In almost half the countries at least two-thirds of expenditures were audited. There is a high correlation between release time and the share of expenditures audited—the more prompt the release time, the higher is the percentage of expenditures audited.

FIGURE 4.8

Legislatures play a minor role in decisions on shifting funds between administrative units in sample low- and middle-income countries

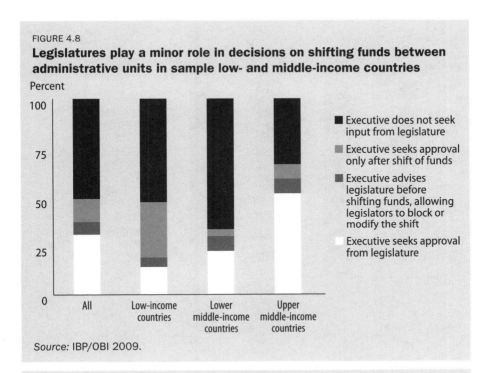

Percent

Legend:
- ■ Executive does not seek input from legislature
- ■ Executive seeks approval only after shift of funds
- ■ Executive advises legislature before shifting funds, allowing legislators to block or modify the shift
- □ Executive seeks approval from legislature

Source: IBP/OBI 2009.

FIGURE 4.9

Budgets of auditing institutions fall short of best practice in sample low- and middle-income countries, 2008 . . .

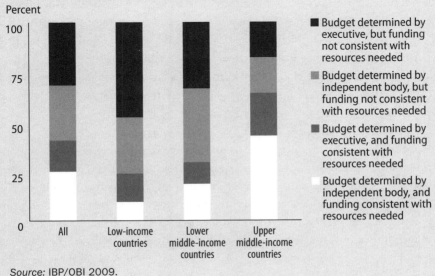

Percent

Legend:
- ■ Budget determined by executive, but funding not consistent with resources needed
- ■ Budget determined by independent body, but funding not consistent with resources needed
- ■ Budget determined by executive, and funding consistent with resources needed
- □ Budget determined by independent body, and funding consistent with resources needed

Source: IBP/OBI 2009.

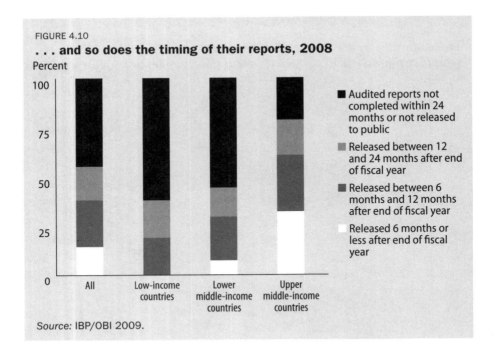

FIGURE 4.10

. . . and so does the timing of their reports, 2008

Source: IBP/OBI 2009.

As a practical matter, there is no acceptable excuse for failing to deliver audited accounts within six months of the end of the fiscal year. The U.S. government, for example, ends its fiscal year on September 30. By law the Department of the Treasury must submit its annual financial report, which is subject to audit by the Government Accountability Office, to the president and Congress no later than six months after that (March 31). To meet this goal, the Office of Management and Budget requires government agencies to observe a 45-day internal deadline, which means that a $3.7 trillion operation is able to close its books for auditing within two months of the end of the fiscal year and deliver a complete financial report four months later.[14]

Performance in opening the budget to evaluation of results is abysmal

Independent monitoring organizations and others face critical obstacles in connecting budget priorities to implementation and results, with perhaps the greatest obstacle being the dearth of information comparing performance with targets. As with the other budget documents discussed in this chapter, lags are common in the release of year-end reports. More problematic, because benchmarks and performance indicators are outlined in neither the budget proposal nor the year-end report, no one—not the executive, legislators, or civil society—can determine the effectiveness of the expenditure program and improve it the next year.

A large gap between allocated and actual funding could indicate a variety of problems with the budget process, including leakage, corruption, and weak forecasting. To monitor these gaps, legislatures and citizens need documents that provide detail on how public funds are allocated and received. This information is not made public in many countries (figure 4.11). Almost two-thirds of low- and middle-income countries in the Open Budget Index sample provided no explanation of differences between allocated and actual spending, or they presented information at such an aggregated level that it would be impossible to determine where the funding gaps were. The problem is even more pronounced when focusing on programs for impoverished populations (figure 4.12). Only 30 percent of developing countries surveyed provided any explanation of the gaps between enacted and actual funding targeted to the poor. In low- and lower middle-income countries three-quarters of the sample provided no explanation of failures in propoor public spending.

As with expenditures, performance targets and outcomes are often left out of year-end reports, depriving stakeholders of the quantitative data needed to assess government performance. In many cases this problem begins at the prioritization stage of the budget process. Most countries (70 percent) in the sample did not present performance indicators in the executive's budget proposal released before the start of the fiscal year (figure 4.13), so stakeholders had no means of gauging the government's performance in public expenditure management. Even countries

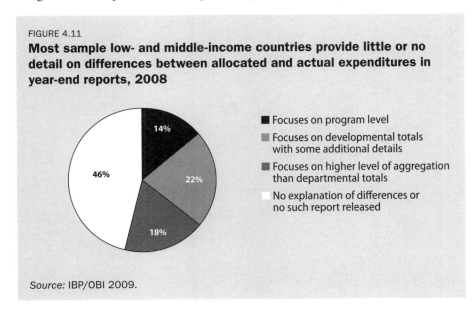

FIGURE 4.11

Most sample low- and middle-income countries provide little or no detail on differences between allocated and actual expenditures in year-end reports, 2008

- Focuses on program level
- Focuses on developmental totals with some additional details
- Focuses on higher level of aggregation than departmental totals
- No explanation of differences or no such report released

14%
22%
18%
46%

Source: IBP/OBI 2009.

FIGURE 4.12

Even fewer sample low- and middle-income countries explain gaps between allocated and actual expenditures to benefit impoverished populations in year-end reports, 2008

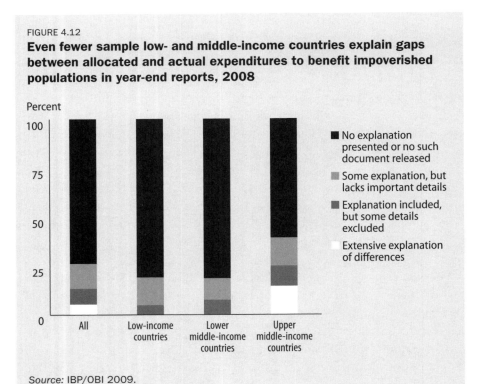

Source: IBP/OBI 2009.

FIGURE 4.13

Few sample low- and middle-income countries include performance indicators in the executive's budget proposal or supporting documents, 2008

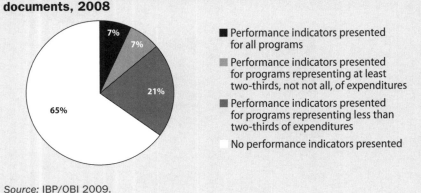

Source: IBP/OBI 2009.

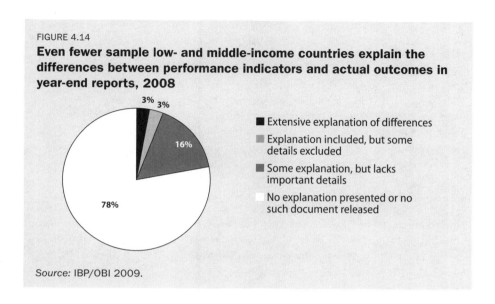

FIGURE 4.14

Even fewer sample low- and middle-income countries explain the differences between performance indicators and actual outcomes in year-end reports, 2008

- Extensive explanation of differences
- Explanation included, but some details excluded
- Some explanation, but lacks important details
- No explanation presented or no such document released

3% 3%
16%
78%

Source: IBP/OBI 2009.

that provided performance indicators did not always explain differences between performance targets and outcomes at the end of the fiscal year (figure 4.14).

Some success stories in budget execution—but more are needed

Although there are substantial barriers to budget transparency in many countries, some countries have achieved considerable transparency. And some countries have successfully reformed their public expenditure management systems to improve budgeting prioritization, execution, and monitoring (box 4.1).

In a large proportion of developing and transition economies, however, civil society organizations and legislatures still face enormous obstacles in holding policymakers accountable for budget decisions. Publication of budget documents is delayed, and in many cases important spending reports are not made public. Furthermore, the budgeting process is overwhelmingly controlled by the executive, with little consultation with the legislature and the public.

Transparency is better at the budget preparation stage, but it is severely lacking at subsequent steps, particularly in execution, monitoring, and learning from results. Governments can hardly expect to improve development outcomes without basic budgetary tools and processes for connecting results to how money is spent. Making these tools available and opening them up to outside scrutiny will increase the amount of noise and criticism governments will have to endure, but it will also help ensure broader understanding of the effort and greater capability to achieve accountability for the scarce resources governments spend.[15]

BOX 4.1
Budget legislation reform in Turkey and Vietnam

In 2003 Turkey passed the comprehensive Public Financial Management and Control Law to establish a far-reaching legal framework for public expenditure management and accountability. The law strengthened strategic planning and performance-based budgeting, multiyear budgeting, and internal budget control and audit systems.

Vietnam also adopted a sweeping budget law in 2002, which clarified the roles and responsibilities of central and provincial governments and conferred new powers on the Provincial People's Councils. Budget plans, budget final accounts for all levels of government, and auditing results must be made public. The Treasury was declared the lead agency in charge of expenditure control and financial management information at all levels of government. The State Audit of Vietnam was charged with conducting external audits of all state budget revenues and expenditures and reporting the results to the National Assembly.

As the Open Budget Initiative notes, expanding on the quotation that opens this chapter:[16]

> The Open Budget Survey 2008, a comprehensive evaluation of budget transparency in 85 countries, finds that the state of budget transparency around the world is deplorable. This encourages inappropriate, wasteful, and corrupt spending and—because it shuts the public out of decision-making—reduces the legitimacy and impact of anti-poverty initiatives. . . .

> Only 5 countries of the 85 surveyed—France, New Zealand, South Africa, the United Kingdom, and the United States—make extensive information publicly available as required by generally accepted good public financial management practices.

> These countries all score above 80 out of a possible 100 points on the Open Budget Index 2008 (OBI). . . .

> The average score for the OBI 2008 is 39 out of a possible 100. This indicates that, on average, countries surveyed provide minimal information on their central government's budget and financial activities.

> Twenty-five countries surveyed provide scant or no budget information. These include low-income countries like Cambodia, the Democratic

Republic of Congo, Nicaragua, and the Kyrgyz Republic, as well as several middle- and high-income countries, such as China, Nigeria, and Saudi Arabia. . . .

Comparisons between the OBI results for 2006 and those for 2008 show that some countries have started to improve their budget transparency over the past two years.

In Croatia, Kenya, Nepal, and Sri Lanka, significant improvements either were influenced by the activities of civil society groups or have created opportunities for greater civil society interventions. Important improvements in budget transparency were also documented in Bulgaria, Egypt, Georgia, and Papua New Guinea. . . .

In short, the new paradigm of expenditure monitoring suggested in this book will not be possible without much higher standards of transparency. Hidden budgets cannot be monitored. Expenditure managers who act in secret cannot be held accountable. Providing for consultation at the beginning of the budget cycle is a good start, and increasingly this is happening. But accountability for results means that processes and reporting during the year need to be open to outside scrutiny, which is problematic in many countries. Providing crucial end-of-year reporting, connecting expenditures to results, encouraging think tanks and universities to evaluate impacts, and making sure audits are completed and scrutinized in a timely manner—these are core accountability routines that are more often ignored than observed in most countries.

Notes

1. Lipscomb and Bergh 1907, p 307.
2. OECD 2001; also see IMF 1999.
3. The details of the PEFA approach are available in PEFA Secretariat (2005).
4. PEFA covers primarily International Development Association–eligible countries.
5. De Renzio 2009.
6. www.globalintegrity.org
7. IBP/OBI 2009. The countries that participated in the Open Budget Initiative are (with the score, out of 100 percent, in parentheses): Afghanistan (8), Albania (37), Algeria (1), Angola (3), Argentina (56), Azerbaijan (37), Bangladesh (42), Bolivia (5), Bosnia and Herzegovina (44), Botswana (62), Brazil (74), Bulgaria (57), Burkina Faso (14), Cambodia (11), Cameroon (5), Chad (7), China (14), Colombia (60), Congo (Dem. Rep.) (0),

Costa Rica (45), Croatia (59), Czech Republic (62), Dominican Republic (11), Ecuador (38), Egypt (43), El Salvador (37), Equatorial Guinea (0), Fiji (12), France (87), Georgia (53), Germany (64), Ghana (49), Guatemala (45), Honduras (11), India (60), Indonesia (54), Jordan (52), Kazakhstan (34), Kenya (57), Korea, Rep. (66), Kyrgyz Republic (8), Lebanon (32), Liberia (2), Macedonia (54), Malawi (27), Malaysia (35), Mexico (54), Mongolia (36), Morocco (27), Namibia (47), Nepal (43), New Zealand (86), Nicaragua (18), Niger (26), Nigeria (19), Norway (80), Pakistan (38), Papua New Guinea (60), Peru (66), Philippines (48), Poland (67), Romania (62), Russian Federation (58), Rwanda (0), São Tomé and Príncipe (0), Saudi Arabia (1), Senegal (3), Serbia (45), Slovenia (73), South Africa (87), Sri Lanka (64), Sudan (0), Sweden (78), Tanzania (35), Thailand (40), Trinidad and Tobago (33), Turkey (43), Uganda (51), Ukraine (55), United Kingdom (88), United States (82), Venezuela (35), Vietnam (9), Yemen (9), Zambia (47).

8. OECD 2001.

9. IBP/OBI 2009.

10. Complete documentation is available at http://openbudgetindex.org/.

11. The country grouping follows the World Bank grouping of countries into six regions. Developed countries are not part of the World Bank regional classification, and they constitute a separate group in the data.

12. World Bank 2007a.

13. There is a high correlation (0.9) between the mid-term review that discusses the changes in economic outlook since the budget was enacted and the one that includes updated expenditure estimates for the budget year under way.

14. There are many problems with U.S. government financial reporting. The information presented here is intended simply to indicate the feasibility of completing and auditing financial statements within a short period. For details of U.S. federal financial reporting, see, for example, www.gao.gov/financial/fy2009financialreport.html.

15. Ramkumar and Krafchik 2005.

16. http://openbudgetindex.org/files/KeyFindingsEnglish.pdf.

Independent monitoring organizations at work

Citizens face significant challenges in trying to monitor government actions, as the Open Budget Initiative data reported in chapter 4 demonstrate. But the emergence of more open societies argues for a complementary form of monitoring by civil society organizations that we have called independent monitoring organizations. Although bottom-up accountability in developing countries is still in its infancy, a framework for accountability, such as the one presented in this book, with government entities acting as agents of citizen-principals, is nonetheless possible.

Independent monitoring organizations have the potential to become agents in making bottom-up accountability work, by turning the free flow of information and mediation between state and society into organized analysis for the purpose of accountability. Independent monitoring organizations and similar organizations are vital for the development of social capital and citizen networks, both core components of a vibrant society that can counterbalance other interests and provide a check on the prerogatives of those holding powerful positions.

This chapter presents an overview of the landscape for independent monitoring organizations—the roles that they can play in ensuring accountability between citizens and the state, what still needs to be done to strengthen them, and lessons for independent monitoring organizations and those supporting them.

What is an independent monitoring organization?

Civil society organizations have proliferated over the past 20 years, particularly in developing countries. India alone has an estimated 1 million or more such groups, and Kenya registers some 250 new organizations each year. Civil society organizations have traditionally acted as substitute service providers, working in the arena between households, the private sector, and the state to negotiate matters of public concern and filling the void left by underperforming or disinterested governments. They have built schools and clinics, supplied microcredit, offered aid and counseling in conflict and disaster areas, and provided many other vital services. Their successes have inspired many of them to aim higher and to involve themselves directly in policy processes at the national and local levels.

This increased activism has coincided with a movement in the international donor community to promote greater civic participation in aid projects and to foster a sense of ownership in developing country communities. Civil society organizations have become focal points in many donors' propoor agendas and frequent recipients of technical assistance and development funds.

Another converging force is the emergence of good governance as a priority among development practitioners. Recognizing that greater spending has not resulted in commensurately better development outcomes, donors and international advocacy groups such as Transparency International have targeted corruption and public sector inefficiencies as obstacles to improving growth and reducing poverty. Governments face greater scrutiny of their policies and greater pressure to demonstrate efficient use of government funds and more effective service delivery. Transparency and accountability have become the watchwords of better governance.

A natural outgrowth of these trends has been the development of independent monitoring organizations, whose mission is to monitor and analyze government policies and services and demand more transparent and accountable behavior. The use of research and evidence-based advocacy by independent monitoring organizations has given them new grounds for dialogue with policymakers and other development agents. These groups have grown in number and sophistication over the past decade with the help of the Open Society Institute, the International Budget Partnership, Revenue Watch Institute, and bilateral donors. Their greater engagement and exposure make this a timely moment for assessing their role in improving transparency and accountability in public spending.

Putting independent monitoring organizations on the map

Measuring the number of independent monitoring organizations is difficult, let alone identifying those focused on particular issues. Many come to budget monitoring or analysis indirectly, through their engagement in more traditional social sector issues or from an advocacy background. The difficulty is compounded by the great numbers of grass-roots organizations that form and disband each year.

Nevertheless, a growing number of independent monitoring organizations are developing a reputation for sustained work on public spending.

Perhaps the simplest measure of their number is the informal network created by the International Budget Partnership to provide training and technical advice to groups engaged in budget work. This network now boasts nearly 100 members from some 80 countries. Revenue Watch Institute has a similar network of partners that pursue its agenda of transparency in resource-rich countries. The Global Development Network includes more than 3,000 organizations engaged in policy research and advocacy, many of them focused on public expenditure management. Transparency International has franchised local chapters around the world and has created dozens of independent monitoring organizations to combat corruption and public spending problems. The Transparency and Accountability Project (TAP), a fairly new effort, has worked with 42 budget and policy-oriented independent monitoring organizations in 26 countries, many of which are part of the International Budget Partnership.

Engaging in a multiagent environment to improve transparency and accountability

Independent monitoring organizations are potentially important nonstate actors in public expenditure management. This section details how they can engage within a multiagent environment to effect positive changes in public transparency and accountability. The framework used here applies multiagency models to describe the functioning of government bureaucracy, with its numerous actors, each with its own interests, capabilities, and responsibilities.

Independent monitoring organizations span a broad spectrum. Individual organizations need to develop a solid basis of relationships with like-minded organizations that may bring different strengths to the table. In a small sample of former grantees from TAP, 10 labeled themselves think tanks, 3 identified themselves as advocacy nongovernmental organizations (NGOs), and 6 were research NGOs or academic research institutions.

Independent monitoring organizations can use this diversity to their advantage. Those with a research focus can collaborate with civil society organizations and grass-roots organizations to direct the attention of other independent monitoring organizations to areas of public spending that may be going off track. Advocacy organizations can develop alliances with think tanks, academic institutions, and quasi-government agencies that also analyze and study public policies and programs. These alliances can go a long way toward forming the groundwork for sideways accountability, as their scholars and officers move in and out of government.

In the routes of accountability depicted in figure 3.1 in chapter 3, independent monitoring organizations belong in the bottom-up accountability segment. But they can also be seen as a link between government entities and those seeking to hold government accountable (figure 5.1). In addition to monitoring government decisions and advocating for improved budgeting, independent monitoring organizations can inform and engage the public to make citizens more effective monitors and relay the needs of the people to policymakers.

Broadly defined then, independent monitoring organizations work with the public as advocates and educators and work with the government as lobbyists. In addition, successful independent monitoring organizations analyze how the public expenditure system is working, where failures exist, and how the failures can be overcome. Four broad categories of actions describe the ways independent monitoring organizations pursue more effective and equitable public spending: gathering budget data, examining spending, recommending solutions, and disseminating findings and advocating for change.[1] During each stage independent monitoring organizations work with the public and the government to inform, engage, and develop ways to improve public resource allocation (figure 5.2).

Gathering budget data
The first step is to compile budget data from various levels of government, service delivery facilities, and external sources. This activity can provide insight into the

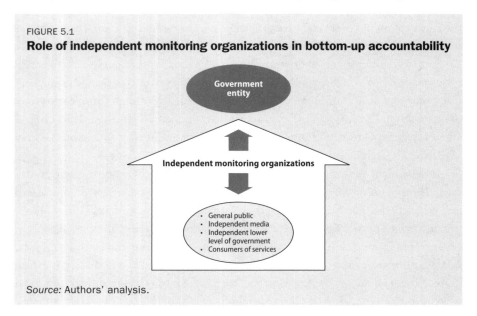

FIGURE 5.1
Role of independent monitoring organizations in bottom-up accountability

Government entity

Independent monitoring organizations

- General public
- Independent media
- Independent lower level of government
- Consumers of services

Source: Authors' analysis.

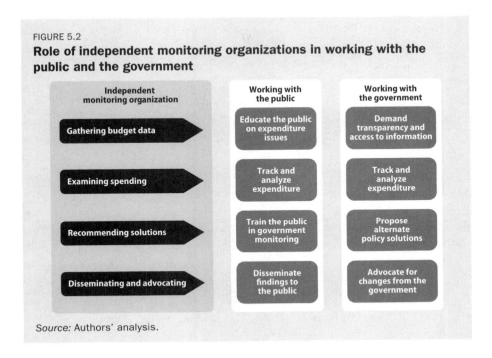

FIGURE 5.2

Role of independent monitoring organizations in working with the public and the government

Independent monitoring organization	Working with the public	Working with the government
Gathering budget data	Educate the public on expenditure issues	Demand transparency and access to information
Examining spending	Track and analyze expenditure	Track and analyze expenditure
Recommending solutions	Train the public in government monitoring	Propose alternate policy solutions
Disseminating and advocating	Disseminate findings to the public	Advocate for changes from the government

Source: Authors' analysis.

transparency of the public expenditure management system and the effectiveness of financial record-keeping policies, particularly at the facility level. Where budget data are available to the public, independent monitoring organizations can use the raw numbers to educate the public about expenditure issues, strengthening their ability to advocate for change and make voting decisions. Where roadblocks impede access to expenditure data from policymakers and civil servants, organizations can use their experience as evidence when lobbying the government for freedom of information laws and other avenues for accessing data.

Educate the public on expenditure issues. Seeing the numbers and understanding the budgeting process can increase the interest of civil society in the budgeting process. Independent monitoring organizations, through targeted education programs, can demonstrate the relevance of the budget to people's daily lives. Public expenditure management is often overlooked, even though the budget may be the most powerful tool a government has for improving the lives of its citizens. Even when information about government policies is publicly available, holding government accountable requires an engaged populace. Budget issues at the central or regional level can seem remote from the daily activities of most citizens. People are keenly aware of shortfalls in service quantity and quality, but they do not always connect their own well-being with expenditure decisions made in the capital.

Public education on the budget is a key component of most independent monitoring organization workplans, and examples abound of excellent and innovative work. One example is the Centre for Budget and Policy Studies (CBPS) in India, which communicates its research findings to district and state politicians but also directs its activities to citizens and advocacy NGOs in its home state of Karnataka.

In 2007 CBPS studied how health and education budgets were allocated across two Karnataka districts with very different socioeconomic profiles.[2] In-depth analysis uncovered disturbing patterns of spending. But even a cursory look at the raw budget data revealed important shortcomings, including a confusing web of budget sources for health and education spending and seemingly overlapping programs such as "additions and alterations," "repair and maintenance," and "school building repairs." The budget data, supported by interviews with officials, also revealed that requests by district officials for reallocations across budget line items had not even been considered by higher level officials. To make the information more accessible and interesting to NGOs and the public, who could lobby district officials for improved spending, CBPS commissioned a film documenting the stages of budgeting in Karnataka. The film is used by service delivery NGOs in Karnataka in developing advocacy strategies on high-priority issues. CBPS also supplies its findings to other advocacy-focused civil society organizations to influence policymakers.

The Institute of Public Finance in Croatia and the Institute for Democracy in South Africa, which publish citizen guides to the budget process, are two other examples of independent monitoring organizations that are encouraging a more engaged and informed public. The guides help civil society understand how public money is being allocated.

The public is not the only audience for education on public expenditures. State officials can also benefit. Legislators are often underinformed about government processes and can benefit from training. Having allies within the government is important for improving government performance and accountability. Developing relationships with government officials who are well versed in budget and expenditure policies can make civic engagement on these issues more effective.

A particularly illuminating example is the evolution of Developing Initiatives for Social and Human Action (DISHA), founded by Madhusudan Devaram Mistry in Gujarat, India, in 1985. During the 1980s, Mistry, a geographer by education, took up the fight for people living in tribal areas in northeastern Gujarat. Over time, DISHA shifted its focus from pure advocacy to "advocacy by the numbers" by delving into state budgets, eventually becoming a source of information for state legislators. Mistry himself was elected to the lower house of the national parliament in 2001 and again in 2004. Although DISHA has maintained its identity as a grass-roots advocacy organization, it has evolved from a pure advocacy organization into an independent monitoring organization (see box 5.1).

Demand transparency and access to information from the government. When independent monitoring organizations begin their research by gathering budget data only to find that the data are not available or are incomplete, organizations often take on a new activity—demanding transparency and access to information from the government. Underlying many citizens' complaints about government is a lack of information about how taxes and other government revenues, such as foreign aid, are being spent.

The reason for this reluctance is clear. Controlling access to information gives governments an edge over people seeking to reform—or simply to complain about—government policies and performance. Governments interested in pursuing their agendas unhindered understand that transparency of information is a necessary condition for accountability. Despite government reluctance in some cases, the momentum behind openness is building. Donors are highlighting the importance of transparency in their projects and grant programs, and citizens are realizing that access to information is a right they cannot afford to ignore. From the mid- to late 1990s the Heavily Indebted Poor Countries (HIPC) Initiative, a debt reduction program, required formal consultations with civil society in the formulation of Poverty Reduction Strategy Papers and the use of debt relief funds (money that would otherwise have been paid to international organizations to repay loans). This innovation sparked an effort to consult with civil society organizations in HIPC beneficiary countries, at least at the planning stage.

In addition to citizen demand for information, government intervention is critical for creating an environment of disclosure and openness, for at least three reasons: "First, only government can compel the disclosure of information from private and public entities. Second, only government can legislate permanence in transparency. Third, only government can create transparency backed by the legitimacy of democratic processes."[3]

Independent monitoring organizations, as intermediaries in the citizen-state relationship, can promote transparency of information by pressuring governments to produce and publish more budget data and more information on their decision-making processes. Independent monitoring organizations have made great strides in opening up government books and disseminating information to the public.

BOX 5.1

**Evolution from advocacy to independent monitoring organization—
Developing Initiatives for Social and Human Action**

M.D. Mistry, the founder of Developing Initiatives for Social and Human Action (DISHA), gave an interview in 2004 that anticipates many themes of this book:

Interviewer: When and why did you find the need to steer DISHA towards budget analysis and advocacy, traditionally the domain of academics and researchers?

Mistry: After a period of struggle to establish the rights of communities living in the tribal areas of Gujarat in the '80s, we realised the need for information on money spent by the national and state governments on tribal development. For years, the Gujarat government claimed large amounts had been spent in tribal areas, but I found no material change in the penurious condition of the tribals and workers I worked with. Where was the money going? So, in the early 90s we gingerly embarked on probing the complexities of the state budget to ferret out figures on expenditure in tribal development schemes.

Interviewer: What were your initial experiences? Were you really equipped for such an exercise, and who were your allies in this effort?

Mistry: The word budget is enough to put off most social activists. Number-crunching is alien territory. Perhaps that is the reason why we received little support from other activists and civil society organisations in the early years. Only a handful of retired bureaucrats, sympathetic to

our cause, led us through the maze of the budget-making process. . . .

Activism, bolstered by this potent tool, has shifted the power dynamics in our favour over the years. All people's movements ought to adopt this route instead of merely limiting themselves to street demonstrations and slogan shouting. If one were to analyse activism in terms of cost-benefit, our route and approach delivers the best results.

. . . When we first saw the budget documents we were overwhelmed. We had to classify the data, scour it for the kind of information we wanted and also try and comprehend the government's accounting system. We had to build our self-confidence and ascertain whether our interpretation of the figures was correct.

We are often surprised by the efficacy of our new-found skills! In one particular year (1997–98) we pointed out 172 mathematical errors in the state budget documents. The same year, we began publishing a series of four-page documents on numerous aspects of the budget, which became an instant hit with Gujarat legislators, especially the opposition that's always on the lookout for sticks to beat the government with. Our much-sought-after notes eventually began to shape budget discussions in the assembly, forcing ministers to reply to pointed queries, all backed by numbers. The secretive apparatus gradually turned more responsive and, above all, the issues of the poor found a place in the agenda of legislators.

Source: Excerpted from Karunakaran 2004.

In Mexico, for example, a coalition of more than 100 politicians, academics, and civil society organizations, referred to informally as Grupo Oaxaca, drafted a freedom of information law and presented it to Congress. Through a well designed advocacy strategy, the group used its political influence to gain a foothold in the legislative process and succeeded in getting the law passed. This national success encouraged other local actors to push for state-level laws. The new laws represented a sea change in Mexican politics, arming citizens with a potent new tool for obtaining more information from the government.

In Rajasthan, India, citizens organized as the Peasants and Labourers Struggle Association (MKSS) had failed to gain access to the state government's rolls on workers' wages. The group pushed for a right to information act in the state and won. Other states were inspired to pass similar laws, and the movement culminated in passage of a national right to information law in 2005 that is now one of the most extensive in the world.

Examining spending

After gathering budget data, independent monitoring organizations can analyze data to reveal evidence of specific misallocations, leakages of funds, and problems with public service delivery. Independent monitoring organizations have many tools at their disposal for conducting these analyses, including adaptations of tools developed and used by the World Bank and others (see box 5.2 and chapter 2). Citizens and government officials can use these analyses to improve public expenditure management systems and service delivery.

The studies highlighted in the following two subsections provided valuable information to the public and the state alike, information that government officials and citizens would have had difficulty uncovering on their own. Even when budget data are completely transparent and available to the public, taking the next step of following the money and how it is spent is often necessary to translate information into results.

Track and analyze expenditures for the public. In many countries the government does not release accurate or timely budget or expenditure data on its own, and when it does the information is often manipulated to show government activities in a better light, as shown in the previous chapter. Sometimes, governments simply lack the resources to rigorously analyze information on public spending. Knowing whether money allocated to certain sectors and facilities actually reaches its destination is critical for assessing government performance, while identifying where and why leaks occur is the first step toward reforming the system.

BOX 5.2
Independent monitoring organizations and other expenditure analysis tools

In addition to Public Expenditure Tracking Surveys, independent monitoring organizations can use tools such as country financial accountability assessments and country procurement assessment reports to improve the efficiency of public financial management systems. A review of these tools by the World Bank in Latin America and the Caribbean highlights recent entry points into procurement and financial management processes by civil society organizations, including these:

- In Honduras the supreme audit institution has begun incorporating results from formal citizen-led monitoring exercises into its auditing of public social sector facilities and has made room for continuing civil society monitoring of implementation of its recommendations.
- In Peru independent monitoring organizations are active in monitoring procurement, providing training on procurement laws, and monitoring procurement through social audits.
- In Guyana, when the government ignored the results of a 2002 Country Financial Accountability Assessment,

civil society and the media pushed the government to implement the recommendations. Over many years citizens have been successful in pressuring the government to implement many of the assessment findings.

In addition to these tools the Public Expenditure and Financial Accountability (PEFA) framework is spelled out and available online, along with completed assessments. A modified PEFA study could be done at any level of government but requires access to government documents and officials. The Open Budget Index is documented online, including the survey instruments and results for each country. Anyone could apply it. Two guides by Ramkumar provide numerous examples of how civil society organizations can develop skills to monitor budgets; how citizen tribunals can expose graft and corruption, particularly in public procurement; how to monitor public infrastructure projects and delivery of textbooks to schools; plus many other home-grown interventions from around the world.

Source: Ladipo, Sanchez, and Sopher 2009; PEFA Secretariat 2005; IBP/OBI 2009; Ramkumar 2007b, 2008.

Expenditure tracking was pioneered by the World Bank in 1996 in Uganda using Public Expenditure Tracking Surveys to identify problems in budget execution, such as delays, leakages, and excessive discretion in allocation (see chapter 2). Similar surveys have been undertaken in other countries. While effective in uncovering deficiencies in the system, the surveys can also be used for ongoing monitoring of government expenditure. Indeed, independent monitoring organizations have implemented their own surveys, focusing on areas thought to be underperforming. These have identified budget execution problems, institutionalized a consistent monitoring process, and built skills in expenditure tracking using an established and well understood methodology.

Three examples show how independent monitoring organizations have analyzed the efficiency of spending in social sector programs that the public strongly suspected were not functioning as they should be. Using adapted Public Expenditure Tracking Surveys and public expenditure analysis methodologies, the Institute for Policy Analysis and Research in Kenya, the Civil Society Coalition for Quality Basic Education in Malawi, and the Bandung Institute of Governance Studies in Indonesia were able to quantify the extent of these problems. By bringing this information to NGOs and citizens, these organizations bolstered the public's ability to advocate for changes based on results and to monitor the impact of government interventions to fix the identified problems.

The Institute for Policy Analysis and Research (IPAR) in Kenya looked at how efficiently the Secondary Education Bursary Fund was operating in Nairobi Province.[4] The program, one of the most important sources of scholarships for youth in Kenya, had a high potential for leakage of funds throughout the expenditure chain, as bursary funds passed through many sets of hands before arriving at their destination. Examining budget records from the Ministry of Education, bursary fund committees, and schools, IPAR was able to quantify the problems that the Kenyan public knew existed—and some that they were unaware of. IPAR's 2006 review of school records showed that only 66 percent of the funds that the ministry reported as going to recipients actually reached them. In some cases, students who were no longer in school were being counted as recipients.

In Malawi the Civil Society Coalition for Quality Basic Education (CSCQBE) conducted three budget monitoring surveys of education expenditures between 2002 and 2007, finding great disparities between urban and rural schools, especially in infrastructure and teacher incentives. Acting on these findings, Parliament stepped up its oversight of the education budget, even creating a subcommittee for budget monitoring. The government also undertook a Public Expenditure Tracking Survey in 2004 to validate the results found by CSCQBE. This work has encouraged the government to reduce urban–rural school disparities in education benefits.[5]

In Indonesia the Bandung Institute of Governance Studies (BIGS) investigated whether three local governments (Bandung, Sumedang, and Banjar) were reaching the benchmarks set by the national government in health and education.[6] BIGS found evidence that program expenditures were well below the nationally legislated minimums in all three municipalities and in the country as a whole. In addition, the data on program spending showed high variability in nonsalary spending on education and health in all three municipalities between 2003 and 2007. The study found that a majority share of nonsalary expenditures was allocated to buildings and infrastructure, so that governments in general were financing only salaries and infrastructure. Nevertheless, in these three communities BIGS found pockets of hope in well run, innovative programs.

These studies were used to advocate for change among government officials and to inform the public about the failures of public expenditure management systems. While it is too soon to know the long-term effects of getting such numbers out to the public, early actions by civil society organizations in these countries paint an optimistic picture. Armed with numbers from IPAR's study, citizens in Nairobi Province are equipped to demand more information from government officials and bursary fund committees and to monitor changes in disbursement. Citizens can use comparisons across cities such as those made by BIGS to push their mayors and other elected officials to perform up to the standards of officials in neighboring cities. While the numbers may not be surprising to citizens, the fact that they were collected by independent monitoring organizations meant that the information reached the citizens and entered the public dialogue, providing one more tool for the principals to use to hold their agents accountable. BIGS coined the term "real" public spending on education and health to denote spending that directly benefits recipients rather than being siphoned off by public sector salaries and investment.

Track and analyze expenditures for the government. Expenditure tracking exercises like those described above can also provide valuable results to decisionmakers. Many policymakers are well intentioned but ignorant of problems on the ground. For these government officials, independent monitoring organizations can act not only as monitors but also as analysts, helping officials make better expenditure decisions.

The Indo-Dutch Project Management Society (IDPMS) in India and the Center for the Implementation of Public Policies Promoting Equity and Growth (CIPPEC) in Argentina demonstrate how expenditure tracking informed government rather than identified glaring examples of corruption. When IDPMS studied the efficiency of public health centers in Karnataka, it uncovered multiple problems, including understaffing, low client satisfaction, crumbling infrastructure, and insufficient spending on pharmaceuticals, resulting in constant shortages of critical medicines.[7] Policymakers acknowledged many of these problems and had even implemented programs such as the National Rural Health Mission to remedy many of them. However, IDPMS's findings quantified the problems in a way that was new to policymakers, estimating the money needed to make five key medicines available to meet patient needs in two districts. Thus, the analysis provided policymakers with information and ideas for improving the functioning of clinics in their state and a quantitative measure of how far they fell below their own norms.

CIPPEC, a respected Argentine think tank, began its 2008 study of teacher absenteeism in Buenos Aires Province with an advantage that many independent monitoring organizations do not have: the respect and ear of the Ministry of Education.[8] Policymakers in Argentina have long turned to CIPPEC for analysis and recommendations on social sector budgeting issues. Starting with anecdotal evidence that teacher absenteeism costs the government large sums in wasted resources, CIPPEC determined that absenteeism was a problem that should be quantified and further explored. While its estimate of secondary school teacher absenteeism (11.5 percent) caught the attention of officials, more important was its analysis of the causes and trends in absenteeism and the finding that absenteeism was more severe in poor areas, information that officials could use to address the problem. CIPPEC's analysis also showed that the requirement that all absences be covered by substitute teachers did little to solve the problem because it was for the most part ignored.

Recommend solutions

The final two actions undertaken by independent monitoring organizations after gathering data and examining spending—recommending solutions, and disseminating results and advocating for change—often completely miss the target in studies conducted by external analysts. When external development agents recommend solutions, they often propose major, costly reforms at the central level—for example, responding to drug distribution problems by reforming central medical stores' procedures, training staff, buying drugs, and investing in buildings and vehicles, a multiyear program with unknown impacts. In contrast, when IDPMS, in the study discussed above, found that clinics had substantially fewer drugs than the government's own standards called for, it recommended financing drugs up to these standards or accepting the medical staff's common behavior of rationing of drugs through partial prescriptions so that most patients received something. A finding of teacher absenteeism might result in donor recommendations requiring substitute teachers, tightening civil service absenteeism policies, or changing remuneration policies for teachers, again with hoped-for impacts but little advance knowledge of effects. The CIPPEC study reviewed above, in contrast, concluded that absenteeism was a behavioral and enforcement problem at the school level and encouraged negotiations among those responsible to solve it.

While there is a place for large-scale reforms—and certainly reforms that change the overall environment and incentive structure are important—independent monitoring organizations rarely operate at that level and can find many small-scale, practical solutions with immediate payoffs that can be implemented quickly if governments at different levels are responsive. Proposing practical, local solutions and following them up with monitoring are core strengths of independent monitoring organizations.

Train the public in monitoring government. An often neglected role for civil society in the budgeting process is monitoring government performance. By making budget data available to the public in easy to understand form, independent monitoring organizations can help make civil society more effective monitors. In addition, many independent monitoring organizations work directly with citizens to develop monitoring tools and to recommend better monitoring methods.

Working in this way can require creative methods targeted to specific groups. In 2008, the Center for Economic Analysis and Dissemination in Paraguay (CADEP) conducted a public expenditure tracking study for primary schools in the capital city of Asunción.[9] Its most striking finding was the near-impossibility for civil society organizations to track funds for education. However, CADEP discovered that there was room for monitoring service delivery and spending once funds reached the facility level. CADEP also found an active group well suited to this monitoring—parent associations. CADEP worked with parent associations to develop posters for schools outlining the main study findings on resource use in schools and on how parents could influence that process.

By working with civil society to improve citizens' abilities to monitor government officials, independent monitoring organizations increase the likelihood of sustainable and long-term monitoring. But they sometimes face challenges from the state in supporting the public's role as government monitor. Particularly in countries where government is disinterested or condones substandard service provision, watchdog groups are vital in identifying and publicizing fraud and corruption that might otherwise go unreported and in spurring governments to reform their practices.

It is also important to understand that government is typically the largest single organization in a country, and it is far from monolithic. Each ministry, agency, and local government unit exercises some independence, has its own purpose and organizational culture, and treats information differently. The prime minister's office and the president's office, as well as the ministry of finance and audit authorities, often have a strong interest in holding sectoral ministries and agencies accountable for results. The same holds true at lower levels of government. Typically, governors and mayors, and their treasuries, are far more interested than are service providers in seeking accountability. Therefore it is important that independent monitoring organizations understand that they may have allies for their work in some parts of government.

In Nigeria the World Bank was selected as a neutral party by the governments of Nigeria and Switzerland to monitor the expenditure of more than $500 million in recovered funds stolen by General Sani Abacha when he was president of Nigeria. The World Bank hired Integrity, a Nigerian civil society organization, to review projects that Nigeria and Switzerland had agreed would be financed by the looted funds. Together with other Nigerian independent monitoring organizations, Integrity reviewed a sample of about 50 construction projects. Integrity's report notes that the looted funds were not segregated but were mixed with regular budget funds (this was later corrected), so it was difficult to trace their use.[10] The report provides a mixed review: a good consultation effort during the preparation of the projects seemed to work, but many problems arose during construction and implementation, more or less mirroring the highly variable performance of the government in all its work. Local chapters of the international NGO Transparency International also operate monitoring projects to curb corruption and see that allocations are appropriately distributed. The infamous Chad-Cameroon pipeline project included monitoring by civil society organizations to determine whether the government of Chad was keeping its commitments.[11]

Propose alternative policy solutions to the government. Independent monitoring organizations can influence budgeting and the effectiveness of spending by proposing concrete and feasible solutions to the state, as well as by recommending solutions to the public. As suggested above, traditionally external agencies have recommended reforms of financial and expenditure systems based on the results of public expenditure reviews and other tools, but such large-scale reforms are difficult to implement. These recommendations often miss small, easily implementable solutions that could affect how well public money is spent. Independent monitoring organizations, in contrast, can combine their local knowledge and understanding of how public services work with the results from gathering budget data and examining spending to recommend simple, targeted solutions. This subsection focuses on recommendations from two independent monitoring organizations, the Center for Democratic Development in Ghana and the National Center for Economic Research in Guatemala, that were particularly inventive and effective.

In a 2008 study of primary school service delivery the Center for Democratic Development (CDD) in Ghana quantified the much discussed but infrequently measured problem of teacher absenteeism, finding that 47 percent of teachers were absent at least one day of the week that researchers visited schools.[12] While that single finding was enough to catch the attention of policymakers and parents alike—not to mention teachers—CDD also took a more in-depth look at absenteeism, hoping to identify causes and potential solutions. A survey revealed that absenteeism spiked on Fridays. Interviews with teachers provided further insight into the reason: teachers reported missing school on Fridays to collect their paychecks and to attend teacher training sessions held at Ghanaian universities. Both activities can require considerable travel. Armed with this information, CDD developed a list of possible solutions, including moving teacher training to later in the day on Saturdays and providing more convenient means of cashing and depositing paychecks.

This book began with the story of the National Center for Economic Research (CIEN) in Guatemala. A major problem that CIEN uncovered in its study of primary school financing programs was not corruption but delays in resource allocation, with critical school resources like textbooks arriving after the start of the school year. CIEN asked follow-up questions of policymakers, service providers, school boards, and service users to determine why the delays were so pervasive. Finding that the start of the fiscal year in Guatemala coincided with the start of the school year, CIEN made a simple recommendation to the Ministry of Education to delay the school year by a month, allowing a lag between the school and fiscal calendars. Officials in Guatemala were drawn to this inexpensive and easily implemented solution. In December 2008, the Ministry of Education reported that it would be moving the school calendar as CIEN recommended.[13]

While many independent monitoring organizations focus on simple recommendations, some organizations have the political clout and experience to propose more extensive reforms. An example is the Research Center of the University of the Pacific (CIUP) in Peru. A 2007 CIUP analysis of national and regional education and health spending in a results-based budgeting initiative in Peru found little relationship between spending and performance on goals for maternal and neonatal health, education, and other social development outcomes. The findings suggested that serious structural changes were needed if results-based budgeting was to have its intended impact. CIUP turned its findings into high-level recommendations for improving an emerging budgeting reform process before the system was implemented fully.[14]

Disseminate findings and advocate changes to the public and the government
The fourth category of action for independent monitoring organizations is to disseminate findings and advocate change. The preceding sections have shown how,

as advocates with the public, civil society organizations, and other groups, independent monitoring organizations can raise awareness of the importance of public spending. Activities can range from conducting simple information campaigns and training in budget literacy to informing voters of the issues, channeling demands from particular groups, and benchmarking state performance. Advocacy provides many opportunities for organizations to engage with both citizens and the government.

Many examples have also been presented of how independent monitoring organizations successfully directed their dissemination and advocacy activities toward the state in ways that the public could not readily act alone. Policymakers have an incentive to deal with organized groups: the costs of screening and sorting individuals are high, so officials can benefit when that task is done for them and when a reputation for quality is established. The implication for civil society organizations is that they, too, need to join the fray (see box 5.3 for various routes to accountability). Part of the task is to ensure that policymakers receive reliable information and that several sides of the arguments are presented for consideration. Independent monitoring organizations can help policymakers screen and sort through demands, acting as a quality filter for the networks that they represent.

Through both state-targeted and public-targeted dissemination and advocacy (see figure 3.1 in chapter 3), independent monitoring organizations have achieved short-term results to problems that other actors in the accountability model have struggled with for decades. While promising, this success raises many questions about independent monitoring organization activity and support in the future, questions examined more fully in chapter 6.

Measuring the impact of independent monitoring organizations— some questions

Independent monitoring organizations are emerging as actors in the accountability model. This chapter has highlighted ways that independent monitoring organizations are working with government, the media, and the public to improve public spending processes and outcomes. However, these initial results should be examined more closely. In particular, questions arise concerning the long-term influence of independent monitoring organizations on public expenditure accountability and how other development agents can extend their influence beyond the short run.

How does context affect an independent monitoring organization's success?

The examples presented in this chapter create an optimistic picture of the influence that independent monitoring organizations can have. However, context is

BOX 5.3
Independent monitoring organizations and other routes of accountability

The main route through which independent monitoring organizations improve transparency and accountability is by influencing government entities or other internal monitors such as citizens through bottom-up accountability (see figure 5.1 at beginning of chapter). Other forms of accountability are also available. Sideways accountability (competition between branches and sectors of government) is another way to influence policy and implementation. Independent monitoring organizations should be prepared to partner with state entities to foster reform and improve outcomes.

Legislatures are a natural ally for independent monitoring organizations seeking to influence the budget and pressure the executive branch to introduce more transparent and equitable practices. Civil society groups often serve as de facto advisors to legislators and support parliamentary committees focused on budget issues. By educating legislators on best practices for budget monitoring and implementation and providing timely information on the budget process and expenditure policies, independent monitoring organizations help to level the playing field for parliaments and the executive, well illustrated by the efforts of Developing Initiatives for Social and Human Action (DISHA) in Gujarat, mentioned earlier in this chapter. In turn, legislators can make data and public officials more available so that independent monitoring organizations can do a better job. These relationships can be mutually beneficial. When the independent monitoring organization produces a successful legislator, as with DISHA's M.D. Mistry, the impact is direct.

Supreme audit institutions are another natural ally within government. Around the world, auditors and independent monitoring organizations are working together to improve accountability and performance. In South Africa the Public Service Accountability Monitor monitors cases of misconduct and the performance of government agencies in Eastern Cape Province, working closely with the legislature to track government responses to financial misconduct and corruption identified in the auditor general's reports.

In the Philippines the national supreme audit institution, the Commission on Audit, partnered with nongovernmental organizations on participatory audit exercises in 2002 focused on performance. Currently, audit officials are cooperating with Procurement Watch Inc., providing access to procurement documents of agencies it is auditing to test a tool for measuring corruption in procurement.

In federal systems, relationships with reformers in one state or region that develop mutual trust and provide access to data can demonstrate to others what might be possible. In a very difficult environment for civil society institutions in the Russian Federation, the Institute for Urban Economics gathered data on central and regional government budgets for health and education in two of Russia's 83 regions in which it had worked previously, the Chuvash Republic and Kaliningrad. It used the data to illustrate some of the benefits of adopting a program- and performance-based approach to budgeting in the expectation that it could then begin to influence other regions and republics to consider similar reforms.

Source: Krafchik and Werner 2004; Ramkumar 2007a; Institute for Urban Economics 2007.

also important. Local conditions may favor or impede such organizations' work in public expenditure management. Several conditions affect how well independent monitoring organizations do their job, influencing both the opportunities for them to flourish and the risks they face:

- *Culture, social mores, and values.* Local customs and traditions may affect how the accountability model works and the role of independent monitoring organizations. For example, it could be particularly difficult in a hierarchical society with a high deference for authority for independent organizations to challenge that authority. Where clan or religious loyalty is strong, independent monitoring organizations might keep a low profile and act unobtrusively. But traditions and cultures change, and some cultures are tremendously adaptive, absorbing a wide range of outside influences. The challenge is to find solutions that work within a given environment, never an advantage of outsiders.

- *Social heterogeneity.* Inclusive societies find it easier to engage in propoor public spending. Societies that are divided along ethical, religious, or social lines will complicate the work of independent monitoring organizations. Budget decisions made in a context of identity politics may be particularly sensitive to analyze and critique. Nor will it be easy to mediate the voices of poor and marginalized people when marginalization stems from institutionalized discrimination. It will be a challenge for independent monitoring organizations to find common ground. Again, however, the example of M.D. Mistry is instructive. DISHA's efforts to support residents of tribal areas in Northeastern Gujarat took off once DISHA began to look at budgets and showed that the issue of tribal rights was one of enforcing budgetary commitments already in the law. In Argentina CIPPEC's finding that teacher absenteeism was worse in poorer schools extended understanding of the problem beyond individual teachers' behavior to the systematic impact they were having on the prospects of poor people in society.

- *Political systems.* A country's political system defines both the statutory parts of the accountability model and the way independent monitoring organizations can operate. Some countries ban NGOs. Some have laws making criticism of the state a crime, while others may strongly discourage it even though it is legal. Those who challenge the state's actions could risk their reputations, relationships, and even livelihoods. The state can use its many powers to coerce and intimidate independent monitoring organizations—or any civil society organization that criticizes the status quo. Depending on the political system, to build a credible reputation, independent monitoring organizations might have to start by concentrating on the mechanical dimensions of budget preparation, classifications, timeliness, and budgetary arithmetic, helping legislators understand the numbers, and leaving the substance of spending decisions to a later date.

- *Legal foundations.* The accountability model presented in this book depends heavily on the ability to create a transparent process in which civil society has the raw material needed to enforce accountability. Particularly important is a legal system that backs up enforcement of laws on access to information and the right of citizens to voice their opinions (box 5.4). If the judiciary is not independent or does not enforce freedom of information laws, the laws will have little impact.

- *Independent media.* Independent information media are vital for openness and transparency and can be important partners for independent monitoring organizations in increasing awareness and shaping public opinion. Independent monitoring organizations would be unlikely to have much impact without a vigorous free press.

BOX 5.4

A legal model encourages civil society participation in Colombia

Colombia enacted legislation in 2003 (Law 850) on the role, rights, and obligations of civil society oversight organizations (*veedurías ciudadanas*). The law grants citizens the right to organize oversight and control bodies and sets out the obligation for public agencies and officials to cooperate with them and facilitate their work. The law also promotes and regulates networks of oversight organizations and creates an institutional support network (the members are the attorney general, comptroller general, government ombuds, and minister of the interior). The law assigns the training of oversight and control organizations to the School of Public Administration. The Administrative Department of the Public Function is responsible for evaluating the program. The Community Participation and Development Fund, administered by the Ministry of the Interior, finances the training of oversight organizations and dissemination of the program.

Program implementation has been slow and difficult, mostly because of a shortage of resources to finance setup and administrative expenses of the oversight organizations. However, there are encouraging signs that the system is gradually taking root across the country. A major risk of the program is capture by local political bosses at the district and town levels for personal political gain.

Source: Ladipo, Sanchez, and Sopher 2009.

How influential are independent monitoring organizations?
Recent data suggest that independent monitoring organizations and civil society organizations generally have not yet meaningfully influenced government policy-making. The creators of the CIVICUS Civil Society Index (CSI) commented on civil society in Sub-Saharan Africa in 2006:[15]

> The impact of civil society on policymaking is particularly limited. In Ghana, for instance, [civil society organizations] have many activities in place to hold the government accountable, but their capacity to influence policy is extremely limited. Although the national budget drafting process in Uganda is consultative, civil society's participation in this area of policymaking is minimal. The few organizations that are involved in the budget process mainly participate in the auditing and implementation stage, but they have little or no input in the drafting process. Overall, civil society operates in a political context where harassment of activists and organizations by state officials is not infrequent. Moreover, the relatively weak institutionalization of the state throughout the territory often provides room for abuse by local leaders and strongmen.

Africa is not alone. Indeed, in every region studied for the index, independent monitoring organizations exhibited limited influence on government policy. In Eastern Europe, where donors have spent large sums to strengthen civil society as a counterweight to the historically strong central government, researchers remarked that interaction between civil society organizations and government institutions "typically consists of various forms of cooperation (often led from above by government) and rarely includes lobbying." Moreover, "when it comes to monitoring government and holding the state accountable on broader policy issues, the overall watchdog and advocacy capacity of [civil society organizations] appears rather low in all countries analyzed here."[16] Of the countries studied, none registered an impact score higher than 2 out of 4, where a score between 1 and 2 reflects no discernible impact to limited impact.

Another index, the Johns Hopkins Global Civil Society Index, used a different methodology in assessing the impact of civil society but reached the same conclusion. Based on a sample of 34 countries, including many Organisation for Economic Co-operation and Development (OECD) countries, the study found an average impact score of just 36 out of a possible 100.[17]

Civil society organizations clearly have a long way to go in establishing themselves as a part of the policymaking process in developing countries. But the 2007

Global Integrity Report notes signs of positive change. It finds that while civil society organizations have difficulty engaging on issues of transparency and anti-corruption, governments are beginning to cooperate on issues of service delivery. Independent monitoring organizations can exert some influence and start the conversation on the importance of public financial management to the performance of government services. Of particular interest is the finding that civil society organizations can more easily engage with governments and exert influence on key decisions of national policy in postconflict situations. This reinforces the notion that the power balance is a key obstacle to independent monitoring organization impact. Weakened state institutions will look to civil society for support in times of crises.

The 2007 Global Integrity Report included special indicators on the effectiveness of civil society organizations in certain African countries. The data suggested that African governments were more willing to cooperate with civil society organizations on issues related to public service delivery than on transparency and government accountability issues.[18] By using governments' growing willingness to engage on these issues, independent monitoring organizations can address transparency and accountability indirectly rather than through a more direct anticorruption approach.

Case studies have also illustrated gains by organizations engaged in budget and public financial management issues. The International Budget Partnership and the Institute of Development Studies at the University of Sussex produced six case studies of groups from diverse environments demonstrating impact in their countries (see box 5.5 on the impact of the Center for Analysis and Research in Mexico).

Hard data on the impact of civil society remain exceedingly scarce, however, largely because the organizations are so new. And their actions tend to be local. The two indices referenced here rely largely on qualitative assessments and case studies to compile their scores. In developing countries few civil society organizations have reached even their 15th anniversary, and many are only a few years old. The focus on transparency and accountability is also new. While it may be too early to assess the impact of independent monitoring organizations beyond the evidence assembled here, that does not mean that the current system of measurement should remain unchanged.

Next steps for independent monitoring organizations

In many ways, the cards are stacked against independent monitoring organizations. Lack of disclosure by public entities severely curtails their ability to monitor public finance. They must raise money outside of government to be plausible monitors

BOX 5.5

Demonstrating the impact of independent monitoring organizations in Mexico

In 2002 the Mexican Chamber of Deputies approved a 600 million peso increase for programs on women's health and related issues. Subsequently, the president of the Budget Committee of the Chamber of Deputies asked the minister of health to divert 30 million pesos to eight nongovernmental Centers to Assist Women. This diversion of funds created an uproar in Congress, as it was clearly arbitrary and irregular. A network of six civil society institutions was formed to address the concern.

Relying on the powers of the independent body established to enforce the 2003 Right to Information Law, the coalition obtained information on the use of these funds. The Center for Analysis and Research (FUNDAR) found that the Centers to Assist Women were linked to Provida, an organization whose activities ran counter to the Mexican government's policies on HIV/AIDS. Some 90 percent of the funds allocated to these organizations was shown to be blatantly misused—most of the payments were not invoiced and went to ghost organizations that shared the same address as Provida. Subsequent investigations by internal and external auditors upheld FUNDAR's findings. The internal auditor imposed a fine of 13 million pesos on Provida, ordered it to return the funds, and barred it from receiving public funds for 15 years.

Source: De Renzio and Krafchik 2006.

of government, often difficult in low- and middle-income countries. Many have their roots in advocacy and single-issue causes, yet monitoring requires specialized analytical capability. Nevertheless, international support for these organizations grows stronger, so the question becomes how best to support their development. The examples in this chapter show pockets of success, although general assessments are less optimistic. The most fundamental support needed from the outside is to pressure governments to become more transparent and to make information available that can be used to monitor governments. International and domestic pressure for governments to open up is therefore the first step. The second step, strengthening independent monitoring organizations, is discussed in chapter 6.

Notes

1. These steps are discussed in detail in Kosack, Tolmie, and Griffin (2010).
2. CBPS 2007.
3. Fung, Graham, and Weil 2007, p. 6.
4. IPAR 2008.
5. Ramkumar 2008.

6. BIGS 2008.

7. IDPMS 2008.

8. CIPPEC 2008.

9. Speratti 2008.

10. World Bank 2006a; Okonjo-Iweala and Osafo-Kwaako 2008.

11. A good starting point on the issues is the World Bank's evaluation of its performance (World Bank 2009a).

12. CDD 2008.

13. Cuevas and Lavarreda 2008.

14. Alvarado and Morón 2007.

15. CIVICUS 2006.

16. Fioramonti and Heinrich 2007, p. 22.

17. Salamon 2004.

18. Global Integrity 2008.

Strengthening independent monitoring organizations

Chapter 5 gave examples of how independent monitoring organizations can play a role in developing policy and improving government programs and operations. When people organize to improve public services, they can have a positive impact—lowering costs for street lights, ensuring delivery of textbooks to schools, or improving service delivery through citizen report cards.[1] Apart from the problem of information availability from governments, independent monitoring organizations face stiff organizational, financing, and development challenges in conducting research and advocating for change.

Within the development community it is widely believed that outside financing and capacity-building assistance can help independent monitoring organizations overcome obstacles such as lack of familiarity with expenditure analysis tools, weak analytical or organizational management skills, and difficulty transforming research into policy change. Such programs—many already in place—are a new area for donors, and ideas on how best to build capacity are still evolving. A limited number of reviews of capacity-building programs provide a start in designing support programs. Good practices such as building interventions on existing capacities and working with organizations that are open to learning and adaptation are lessons that apply to any capacity-building program.[2]

This chapter uses information on the experiences of independent monitoring organizations and of organizations participating in the Transparency and Accountability Project's small grants program to begin to understand their capabilities and needs. The information comes from two small nonrandom samples of 34 independent monitoring organizations. Until systematic evaluation evidence is available on donor efforts to strengthen such organizations, this is the only empirical data at hand. It is used here to present a few lessons that the organizations and donors might consider as this area of activity expands.[3] Box 6.1 offers the perspective of Nigeria's former minister of finance on the role of civil society organizations in the budget process during 2003–06.

Characteristics of a small group of independent monitoring organizations

Independent monitoring organizations are in their infancy. They have a long way to go to reach their full potential in holding governments accountable and influencing development outcomes. The grandmother of modern think tanks, the Brookings Institution, was founded in 1916. In its lifetime it has been instrumental in advocating for important accountability and financial management functions in the U.S. federal government, such as the U.S. Bureau of the Budget in 1921 (now the Office of Management and Budget) and the Congressional Budget Office in 1971. Other well known independent think tanks and advocacy groups in the United States are much younger, including the American Enterprise Institute (1943), the Rand Corporation (1946), the Urban Institute (1968), and the Heritage Foundation (1973). The Center on Budget and Policy Priorities, the U.S. equivalent of an independent monitoring organization and parent of the International Budget Project, was started only in 1981. Think tanks and independent monitoring organizations are even newer phenomena elsewhere in the world, and it is no accident that the oldest ones in developing countries date only from the late 1980s.

Organization and management

Young organizations need time to develop, but outside help and exposure to the practices of similar organizations can speed the process. The information in this section comes from the first round of the Transparency and Accountability Project (TAP), which surveyed 14 independent monitoring organizations receiving grants in 2006 and 2007 as part of the pilot testing of a small grants program. Organizations were asked about the following seven organizational management categories: personnel management, personnel incentives, training policies, financial and general management, quality control, dissemination, and performance tracking of the impact of communications (see box 6.2 for summary results and descriptions of the indicators). The results show how survey information can be used to describe institutional development status.[4]

BOX 6.1

Reflections of former Nigerian Minister of Finance Ngozi Okonjo-Iweala on civil society organizations in the 2003–06 budget process

In Nigeria we have the kind of budget process that obtains in many African countries. We have the drafting stage, the legislative approval, the implementation stage, and then the monitoring stage. At each stage there is a potential for civil society organizations to participate to make the process more transparent. But actual participation was really only in one area.

We typically start with a discussion with the president where he gives his ideas of priorities, size, and, parameters, and we discuss with the director of the budget office and the team from the Ministry of Finance. We then attempt to put together a draft approach to the budget, which we call a "Fiscal Strategy Paper." Essentially, we set out the parameters and the directions of the budget and the potential tradeoffs that we have to make in financing the budget.

After this initial process we typically would consult the legislature and civil society, to get their inputs, and also to draw in the spending agencies to give inputs on whether the directions and the parameters and so on were correct. And we often got very robust comments back—mostly criticisms—but which we found very helpful.

We would take these comments into account, revise the budget, debate in cabinet, and then send the budget, after the president had approved it, to the legislature. And here we would have a very tough time, because this was the time for horse trading. As you know, in many countries this is the time for legislators to try to insert their pet projects into the budget.

But we thought that there was a chance for civil society to also participate actively. If we had cooperated well with civil society, they could have helped us in lobbying some of the parliamentary members, to say,

"Look, keep a focus on these priorities. This is important. We must give more to health, or to roads, or to water—whatever priorities had been decided on." But for our part, as Ministry of Finance, I don't think we made the kind of effort needed. I think we were overwhelmed in trying to put things right. But we could have made a better alliance and had them help us lobby to maintain focus.

And then, in implementation of the budget, working with the sector spending agencies and departments, a very important role for civil society organization is to see what's really going on, and how the budget is being spent. And at the end of the budget cycle we introduced a budget implementation report which hadn't existed previously. And civil society would have a big role to play in that. But, again, I would say that there was more interaction with civil society at the front end and not as much at the back end. But clearly there is a need for that to happen.

Often, once the budget was passed and implemented, rather than being allies we had a lot of antagonism with civil society, because they would actually come out and say, "Oh, the Ministry of Finance has done this or taken away money from this area," or "They are lying. They haven't put as much money in this area," and so on. And, you know, we could have had much more productive relationships. But I found that often the civil society organizations did not possess the kind of knowledge and expertise that made them really good critics of the budget process.

Civil society organizations in Nigeria tended to concentrate on the federal government and the federal budget, and they rarely went to the provinces or to the local governments or states to ask questions. So it was a big frustration to me—why this focus on the Ministry of Finance? Why not

(continued)

BOX 6.1 (continued)

Reflections of former Nigerian Minister of Finance Ngozi Okonjo-Iweala on civil society organizations in the 2003–06 budget process

go to even the other ministries? There was a huge missed opportunity. And it's one of the places where we can build substantial capacity for civil society organizations.

First of all, the civil society organizations that we dealt with I felt didn't have very clear objectives. It wasn't clear what they were interested in. Was it about tackling corruption and patronage? Was it about assuring a better allocation of resources to certain sectors? Was it about supporting certain marginalized groups? What was really the objective? It wasn't always clear to me. At the end of the day, I think they were more about the idea of having more information and more transparency of accounts. This issue of what is the objective of the civil society group is critical. And it's the first thing that civil society groups should get clarified.

The other issue was technical competencies. There was a group of nine civil society organizations that worked more closely with me on this budget, monitoring and enhancing transparency. But there was a very different level of skills. I felt that many of them just didn't understand the budget process, didn't have the skills to make really good and critical comments. So if we are to have civil society organizations do the kind of engagement to enhance transparency that we want, we really need to find a way to up their skills.

On effective communication strategies: We had a few times when they gave press conferences. And the information being put out wasn't right—in spite of having spent some time with them, in spite of having made information available. So, again, what are you really trying to achieve? And how can you communicate effectively to push your purpose forward?

On dialogue with the authorities: I used to hear, "We always have difficulty

accessing information." "Oh, but you're not accessible." "It's difficult to see you." And I admitted that. We could have done better to make a team within the ministry that would constantly engage with them. I did have a civil society coordinator, but I guess the effort wasn't enough. So we take some of the blame. But if ministries of finance and civil society organizations are to work well on budget issues, there needs to be a concerted effort on both sides for a continuous dialogue.

If civil society organizations are to play this kind of role, how do they get funded? We struggled with this in Nigeria. Many of the organizations did not have adequate funding, and they were torn. Sometimes they said, "Give us part of the budget, you know, to help us." And then the next minute they said, "No, maybe you shouldn't. People will think we've sold out." So I could see them struggling with this issue. And I think this is where donors really need to step up. And I'm glad to say that there's an effort now by donors to fund this kind of thing.

There is no point sending organizations from outside to come and monitor. They will never do the same kind of job that indigenous civil society organizations will do. So it's better to spend money training civil society organizations in the countries and getting them to do the monitoring than to have support organizations out here do it. Or at least there should be partnerships between civil society organizations out here and those in the countries. If we are serious about improved governance in our countries, improved transparency, then we really need to set to work on this area.

Source: A lightly edited and shortened version of the transcript in Brookings Institution (2007). See also, Okonjo-Iweala and Osafo-Kwaako (2008).

BOX 6.2

Summary results and institutional management indicators in the Transparency and Accountability Project

The indicators cover the following elements (see figure):

Personnel management. Specification of job responsibilities and qualifications, standardized performance evaluation system, employee opportunities to describe and discuss accomplishments, formal orientation program, and resources allocated to organizational development.

Personnel incentives. Formal career ladder, opportunities for staff to publish in own name, mid-level staff participation in external meetings, formal orientation program for new employees, and training for existing employees.

Training policies. Formal training for existing employees, formal in-house training events, training when staff assigned to a new area, and training budgeted annually.

Financial and general management. Training allocations in annual budget, tracking of direct and indirect costs, tracking of individual project expenditures, tracking of status of grants and contracts, frequency of independent audit, development of annual budget, allocation of resources to organizational development, tracking of timely delivery of project outputs to clients, tracking of projects with cost overruns, and tracking of repeat clients for grants and contracts.

Distribution of scores for 14 independent monitoring organizations on seven institutional management indicators (percent)

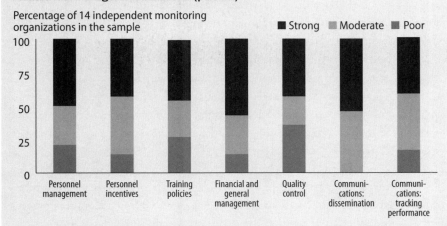

Note: Scores, which range from 0 to 1, reflect performance on the underlying questions for each characteristic. Scores are scaled from 0 to 100 percent in the figure. Missing observations are excluded. Of the total sample of 14, 3 organizations did not respond on training policies, 1 on dissemination, and 2 on tracking communications performance. *Source:* Struyk 2008.

(continued)

BOX 6.2 (continued)
Summary results and institutional management indicators in the Transparency and Accountability Project

Quality control. Peer review of externally disseminated publications, formal and written peer review policy, standards specified for peer review process, and peer review comments provided in writing.

Communications management, dissemination. Preparation of formal communications strategy, specification of target audiences for major projects, adjustment of format and content of materials to reflect intended audience, communications budget

for major projects, monitoring of communications effectiveness, number of staff members primarily responsible for external relations, publications available on organization's website, and use of email alerts.

Communications management, performance tracking. Tracking of website activities, presentations by staff members, press coverage of or by staff members, publications output and number of publications sold, and distribution of evaluation forms at events.

For most indicators about half the organizations have scores in the highest range (0.81–1.0), meaning that a substantial share scores well in each category. These 14 independent monitoring organizations have relatively strong practices for personnel incentives, financial and general management, and dissemination. The generally high scores for financial management cover preparing an annual budget, tracking a range of expenditures, working with grants and contracts, and undergoing regular external audits. The organizations are strongest on dissemination, likely reflecting the fact that many come from an advocacy background.

While caution is required in interpreting the results from such a small sample, they do suggest areas needing improvement. One organization scored in the highest range on all indicators, and two did so on six of the seven indicators. At the low end of the spectrum, two organizations never scored in the highest range, and three scored in the highest range on only one indicator. The differences are particularly large for management practices.

This review suggests that it is straightforward to benchmark organizations and help them target obvious weaknesses relative to their peers. Because the ratings correspond to specific practices, many problems can be fixed by changing practices and behavior, although some problems are related to resource constraints.

Age, size, funding, and use of time

The remainder of the chapter is based on a second sample of 20 independent monitoring organizations in Africa, South Asia, and East Asia. These organizations participated in a subsequent grant round and in a baseline survey of their capabilities as part of a planned evaluation of the TAP. It is also a small sample, but it covers a different set of questions and provides substantial information about the organizations.

Eight of the organizations are less than 10 years old, eight are 10–14 years old, and four are 15 years old or older. Five consider themselves think tanks or research NGOs, and the rest are either advocacy nongovernmental organizations or another type of civil society organization. About half spend 75 percent or more of their time in advocacy work, and the other half spend 60–75 percent of their time in research. Only one organization characterizes itself as doing mostly in-depth quantitative policy analysis; most of the others do primarily qualitative analysis. Participation in TAP requires that the organizations complete a quantitative analysis, so this is a learning and development opportunity for most of them. The expectation is that they are seeking to change how they spend their time and develop new capabilities and audiences in the process.

The organizations are small. Fourteen have fewer than 10 full-time analysts. On average they have 19 full-time staff of any type, including analysts, and 7 part-time staff. The larger organizations (those with more than 10 full-time analysts) have 41 full-time staff and 9 part-time staff on average.

About 70 percent of funding comes from outside sources—from grants and contracts from international foundations and agencies (figure 6.1). The larger organizations get about 20 percent of their funding from domestic foundations and more than 30 percent from domestic resources. The smaller organizations have little access to domestic grants but still receive about 30 percent of total revenue from domestic contracts and fees. Thus it appears that these independent monitoring organizations would not exist without external support, or they would be much smaller than they are today. While there is the potential for their work to be heavily influenced by outside agencies, more than 75 percent of the projects of the smaller organizations were financed with unrestricted funds in 2008, a high level of autonomy, and just under 50 percent of the projects of the larger organizations. It is not surprising that these organizations, like their governments, enjoy considerable outside support at this stage of development. The picture is likely to be substantially different in 20 years.

Analytical staff spend about 80 percent of their time on five activities: 27 percent on research and analysis, 17 percent on education and training events, 14 percent on delivering conferences and workshops, 14 percent on other general advocacy work, and 10 percent on providing technical assistance to government agencies. This allocation is heavily weighted to outreach. All but one organization

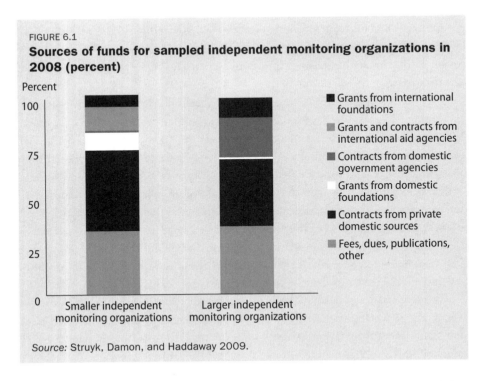

FIGURE 6.1

Sources of funds for sampled independent monitoring organizations in 2008 (percent)

Source: Struyk, Damon, and Haddaway 2009.

were involved in some type of government accountability work in 2008, and that work accounted for just under half of all projects.

In short, these are relatively young organizations, most with their roots in advocacy related to government accountability. There is little question that they are participating in the competitive grants program to strengthen their analytical and quantitative skills. They depend heavily on international organizations for financial support, but it is encouraging to see that a nontrivial share of their revenue is from domestic sources.

Quality assurance for data gathering and analysis

TAP's small grants program designed its requests for proposals with the expectation that each organization could complete data gathering and the initial analysis in about five months. From the outset the major impediment for participating organizations was developing and following a detailed analysis plan that would allow them to complete the work as intended. Timing was critical, because all participating organizations, which were scattered across the world, needed to complete their work on the same timetable so that they could meet to peer review each other's efforts. In the first round of grants, completion had been scattershot, with the first drafts delivered barely in time for the peer review meeting, followed by a feverish effort during the three-day meeting to prepare what was in all cases a vastly improved second version.

As a result, for subsequent competitive rounds the project provided more structure, standardized the analytical task (while leaving the topic open), and expanded the requirement for up-front planning even at the proposal response stage. In addition, organizations discussed their work plans with project staff several times in the early stages of the work. The impact in the second, third, and fourth rounds was a vast improvement in the organizations' ability to complete the work to an increasingly high degree of quality well before the peer review meeting.

One organization indicated that it nearly did not apply to participate because the type of work being proposed usually took two to three years to complete. The staff were astonished to discover the work could be completed in just five months. Combining speed with quality is particularly important for independent monitoring organizations because work must be timely to influence the annual budget process, which follows a brief calendar of only a few months. Achieving higher quality during that window largely determines the organization's reputation and whether anyone pays attention to its analysis and suggestions.

Often, descriptive data suffice to show empirically what is going on with money flows. These are monitoring organizations, after all, not evaluation organizations. Nevertheless, data collection needs to be done carefully, sample sizes must be adequate, and standard statistical tests should be applied to determine whether observed differences in sample means for subgroups are random or have a high probability of reflecting true differences.

Characterizing correlations as causal relationships and overinterpreting data are other basic pitfalls that must be avoided—but often are not. Deflating expenditures to compare real values over time is a basic procedure, often neglected. Running regressions without understanding the underlying theory creates problems that are immediately obvious to many intended recipients of the work. To be credible, independent monitoring groups do not need to do the most advanced work, but they do need to be careful and timely. Simple analytical techniques can go a long way in monitoring work, especially if the topic is narrow and carefully chosen and the data are well suited to the topic.

In short, a strong reputation for high quality and timely analysis is important for the credibility of independent monitoring organizations. The baseline survey of organizations found that seven have comprehensive, apparently effective, quality assurance processes. Another seven have good basic systems that could be improved; and four "need lots of work."[5] As with management practices, quality assurance often requires changes in practices, although many of the changes have cost implications.

Communications and advocacy

In contrast to the analytical side, TAP grantees have considerable strengths in communications and advocacy, particularly the organizations with advocacy backgrounds. Nevertheless, they have benefited from exposure to the practices of other similar organizations and modern techniques for tracking potential clients and impact.

The baseline survey of 20 organizations in 2009 provides considerable information about how they communicate and how they are perceived. Organizations were asked about how they tried to influence policy on a "hot topic"—a current policy issue on which the organization has results and a position to contribute. The favored means are to bring pressure through the press and to try to influence policymakers directly through public and private forums (figure 6.2).

The organizations were also asked to rate the importance of different audiences on a scale of 1, least important, to 5, most important (figure 6.3). Although the average score for all organizations was higher than 3.4, their focus is clearly domestic, as international organizations and foundations rank lowest. The rankings of domestic audiences are extremely close but suggest that communicating to the public and to other NGOs that specialize in advocacy—indirect methods of reaching officials by inspiring others to make noise—are at least as important as directly

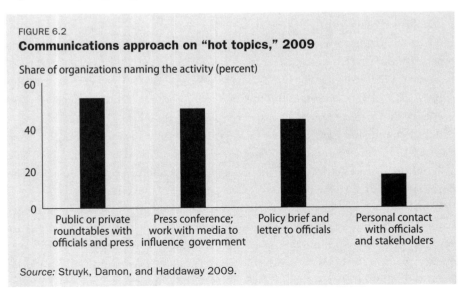

FIGURE 6.2
Communications approach on "hot topics," 2009

Share of organizations naming the activity (percent)

Source: Struyk, Damon, and Haddaway 2009.

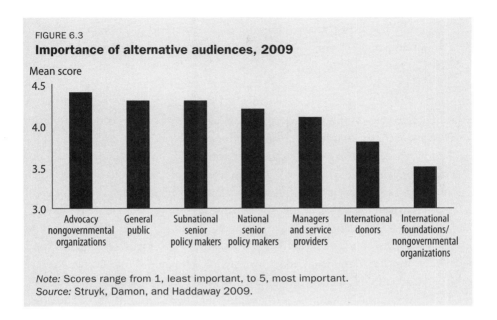

FIGURE 6.3
Importance of alternative audiences, 2009

Mean score

Note: Scores range from 1, least important, to 5, most important.
Source: Struyk, Damon, and Haddaway 2009.

influencing local and national policymakers. In other responses, about half the organizations said that they develop a communications plan even before they begin the analysis. The other half waits for the results or allows ideas on communications to evolve during the project. Almost two-thirds regularly work with networks of other civil society groups to disseminate their findings and press for action.

Finally, the independent monitoring organizations were asked to rate how receptive national and local administrations and parliamentary groups were to analytical inputs, both now and two years earlier. Nearly two-thirds thought there was little or no receptivity at the national level two years ago, but by 2009 more than half the sample thought that the situation had moved to neutral or better. Receptivity of regional and local governments was assessed as quite low, but it also improved a bit.

A "policy community" survey received responses from 316 knowledgeable individuals who were familiar with policy formulation in the countries in which the independent monitoring organizations are located. By country, the sample size ranges from 9 to 63. This group basically agreed with the organizations' assessment that at the national level just over half of government officials and members of parliament were neutral or willing to accept analytic inputs from think tanks and research-advocacy organizations in 2009, although the share varied widely across the 11 countries in the sample. Interest by government officials was assessed as lowest in Cameroon and highest in Kenya.[6]

These respondents also rated various information sources, including the independent monitoring organizations, on the use and quality of the information being provided to the policy community. Respondents rated each source as a primary, secondary, or tertiary (used only occasionally) source, or assigned a zero for not used at all. The rankings show a preponderant use of the Internet and of government ministry or agency information (figure 6.4). A substantial share of the respondents are from government agencies, so the finding on government information is no surprise.

More of a surprise is the finding on the role of the Internet and local organizations. More than likely, 10 years ago the Internet would not have even shown up among the answers in these countries. That it ranks first today is consistent with the assertion in chapter 5 that this technology is a game changer for governments (along with democracy and cell phones). Similarly, local think tanks and local advocacy organizations essentially rank even with international organizations like the World Bank and the United Nations Development Programme, another measure of the profound change that has taken place.

International agencies are rated highest for quality, just slightly above the Internet (see figure 6.4). Local think tanks are even with the government and well above advocacy civil society organizations, research institutes, and professors. For relevance or applicability, international agencies lose their advantage, but advocacy groups and researchers remain lower than the other options—professors may be a

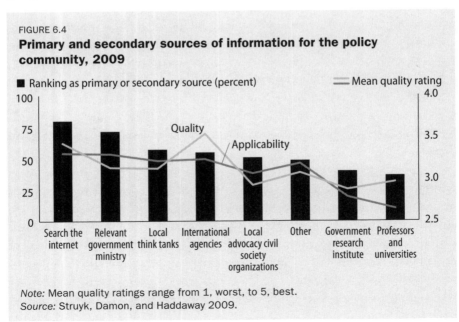

FIGURE 6.4

Primary and secondary sources of information for the policy community, 2009

Note: Mean quality ratings range from 1, worst, to 5, best.
Source: Struyk, Damon, and Haddaway 2009.

little out of touch, but presumably advocacy organizations are less relevant because they tend to be focused on narrow issues. The challenge for advocacy organizations is to move toward becoming think tanks or to partner with think tanks to improve the quality and relevance of their work. Local think tanks will top international organizations as they gain access to the same information, improve the quality of their work, and plug into the policy process. The main lesson here is that all these changes can be made. The next section is about support for doing so.[7]

Actions taken to strengthen independent monitoring organizations

Many capacity-building programs have tried to address these points. Most efforts fall into two categories: thematic programs providing assistance in the context of a donor effort focused on monitoring government spending or revenues in some way, and programs providing assistance independent of a particular thematic focus. Both types give priority to partner organizations with a positive influence on policymaking. Nonthematic programs generally view capacity development as a tool for broadly improving policymaking, while thematic programs are concerned more with improving decisions in a particular area, such as budget or expenditure transparency.

While capacity-building programs can shed some light on the efficacy of different models of providing support to independent monitoring organizations, comparing their effectiveness is difficult because program evaluations have been limited, and for capacity-building programs that have been evaluated, evaluation types have differed. Some have had only process evaluations, which document how well the program operated. Others have had impact evaluations of one type or another. Some of these have assessed the impact of operational efficiency on participating organizations' ability to do good work; others have identified overall program impacts, particularly on policymaking. A common characteristic of all these evaluations is that they are purely ex post because no baseline data were collected. Thus, results are more impressionistic than rigorous.

Despite the limited evidence from evaluations, a review of major capacity-building programs provides some insight into the characteristics of a successful program. Five programs stand out. They include two thematic programs (the International Budget Partnership and Revenue Watch Institute) and three nonthematic programs (a United States Agency for International Development Policy Research Organizations program in Bosnia and Herzegovina and partially replicated in Azerbaijan, the International Development Research Centre's Think Tank Initiative, and the Secretariat for Institutional Support for Economic Research in Africa; see box 6.3 for details).[8]

BOX 6.3
Examples of capacity-building programs for independent monitoring organizations

The *International Budget Partnership* has worked since 1997 with civil society organizations to provide a network of support to members through meetings, training, and technical and advocacy resources. In 2004 its Civil Society Budget Initiative began to operate a grant program for partners and to provide some long-term institutional support for carefully selected partners. This book refers repeatedly to the International Budget Partnership and uses its Open Budget Index data extensively.

Since 2002, *Revenue Watch Institute* has promoted responsible management of oil, gas, and mineral wealth for the public good—first as part of the Open Society Institute and since 2006 as an independent nongovernmental organization. It supports local and international civil society organizations through grants, training, and mentoring to build grass-roots organizations that monitor revenue flows from extractive industries and government expenditures of these funds. It also presses for greater openness and better use of funds. Its partners are prominent implementers of the Extractive Industry Transparency Initiative.

The Urban Institute implemented the *Policy Research Organizations project in Bosnia and Herzegovina* from 2003 to 2007 with United States Agency for International Development funding. It aimed to strengthen think tanks by providing research grants through a noncompetitive application process and offered a range of other support activities, including training and research mentoring.

The *Secretariat for Institutional Support for Economic Research in Africa* was created in 1997 and implemented by the International Development Research Centre through 2004. Its goal was to strengthen promising think tanks in Sub-Saharan Africa. It had 10 full-partner think tanks and 6 with looser connections. The program provided core funding and a range of training and mentoring support.

The International Development Research Centre subsequently launched the *Think Tank Initiative,* which issued its first call for expressions of interest in 2008 from 11 countries in East and West Africa. It was overwhelmed by more than 300 proposals. Twenty-four grants were made in East and West Africa. A second call was issued in 2009 for 12 countries in Latin America and South Asia, with results to be announced in mid-2010. This is a large-scale initiative with a long time horizon. It received an initial $100 million commitment from the Hewlett Foundation over 10 years and additional financial support from the International Development Research Centre and the Bill & Melinda Gates Foundation.

The *Transparency and Accountability Project* (TAP), with initial support from the Hewlett Foundation, has assumed that organizations would have core support from other partners and so has focused on developing expenditure monitoring skills and advocacy through a learning by doing and peer review process. It issues requests for proposals that are structured around tools rather than topics, asking for responses that apply these tools to a domestic expenditure issue in health or education that is a high priority for policymakers.

BOX 6.3 (continued)

Examples of capacity-building programs for independent monitoring organizations

These projects generally last about nine months.

TAP's focus on tools has a longer term counterpart in a program managed by the Global Development Network, with technical support from the Results for Development Institute, funded by the U.K. Department for International Development. The program, *Strengthening Institutions to Improve Public Expenditure Accountability,* has begun working with 15 competitively selected independent monitoring organizations in Africa, Asia, and Latin America. These organizations,

in tandem, are undertaking a rigorous five-year program of applying program budget analysis, benefit-incidence analysis, and cost-effectiveness analysis to national expenditures in education, health, and water. Their expenditure data are updated annually, and the groups will develop fully costed proposals for reform that will use these same techniques to simulate the impacts of the proposed reforms.

Source: Struyk 2008; http://.tap.resultsfordevelopment. org; www.gdnet.org/cms.php?id=grp_details&grp_ id=13; Miller 2007.

These programs exhibit the following attributes that many donors agree are required to achieve substantial and sustained effects:

- A focus on organizations, not individual scholars.
- Institutional development as an explicit program element.
- Sufficient consistency in approach across organizations so that a distinct pattern of support can be defined.
- Multiyear provision of financial and other assistance.
- Execution in more than one country.

For review, the programs are divided by the type of support provided: financial and technical.

Financial support

Although some of the organizations participating in TAP are partly supported by government contracts, independent monitoring organizations are generally reluctant to receive funds from government agencies and international organizations such as the World Bank, which could compromise their independence (see box 6.4 for a discussion of experience with funding civil society organizations in India). Their natural financial partners are other civil society organizations and foundations; those with significant amounts of money for this purpose tend to be located in high-income countries (this is clear from the initiatives in box 6.3; even if funded by governments, the money tends to be channeled through independent

BOX 6.4
Observations on the funding history of civil society organizations in India from Vinod Vyasulu, founder of the Center for Budget and Policy Analysis in Karnataka, India

What about funding of CSO [civil society organization] activity? This is a complex issue. There are CSOs that completely reject funding from governmental, and foreign, sources.

A good example is the Mazdoor Kisan Sangharsh Sanghatan (MKSS or the Peasants and Labourers Struggle Association) or the Wada na Todo Abhiyan (WNTA or Don't Break Your Promise Campaign). They feel that the advantage from receiving such funds is more than offset by potential conflicts of interest as they take up various causes. They work only with individual contributions from members and friends of the movement.

There are other CSOs that reject foreign funding but accept money from governmental agencies. Money from foreign sources may distort priorities; hence it is better to refuse it. Government money, on the other hand, comes from the Indian taxpayer and should be used to fight for his causes. The Council for Advancement People's Action and Rural Technology (CAPART) is a union government agency

that funds CSOs. It is also true that there has been tension between CAPART and CSOs on many issues: CAPART has even published a "blacklist" of NGOs!

Many of the CSOs engaged in research-based advocacy work with funds from foreign donors. They try to work with multiple donors so that they are not dependent on any one. If such an agency is happy to fund work that the CSO defines, they have no problems in accepting it. There is no question of influencing the agenda or of any kind of subversion as such foreign funds can only be accepted after government permission under the Foreign Contributions Regulation Act, under which many of these CSOs are registered. This act is currently being strengthened.

To date, there is very little in the nature of Indian philanthropy. With Indian firms succeeding on the global scene, perhaps in the near future this is an avenue that will open up. The debate goes on.

Source: Excerpted from Vyasulu (2008).

organizations). Building up a new organization takes time and enough money to provide a career path that can attract and retain professionals.

The Africa Capacity Building Foundation, now 20 years old, is not included in this review because in its first 15 years it supported the development of economics capacity in ministries of finance, central banks, universities, and think tanks (both independent and connected to the government) focused almost exclusively on macroeconomics, trade, taxation, fiscal policy, monetary policy, and economic analysis—hard core economic knowledge and research at an advanced level. It has contributed to a notable improvement in technical economic skills inside and outside of ministries of finance and central banks in Africa. Its model of support for most of its history has been general grants supporting the development of the targeted institutions, and the support has been long term.[9]

The first five programs described in box 6.3 have followed this model for the most part, providing multiyear funding for analytic or research projects and core support. Typically, the programs require an annual business plan or research plan, which is reviewed, critiqued, and funded. The programs provide technical assistance and supervision to help the organizations they support succeed with their plans. The Think Tank Initiative follows this approach with three variations on core funding tailored to the capacity of its partners. Core support comes in the form of multiyear grants for expenditures and associated overhead costs that ensure funding to develop and execute a coherent policy research and advocacy agenda and to adjust the agenda to changing circumstances, such as government priorities. Because not all partners are ready for full responsibility from the outset,[10] a two-tier grant structure gives the most capable partners full control of allocations, guided by agreed-on benchmarks for organizational performance, while partners with less organizational capacity work more closely with the project secretariat on funding decisions.

Technical support

In addition to financial support, each capacity-building program provides technical support to improve research and analytic capacity, communication of results, advocacy of improvements, and effectiveness of the organization.

Comparing programs is difficult because of differences in the environment in which programs have been implemented; the effectiveness of the implementing organization in executing the program, including how well it motivated partner organizations to take advantage of the program's developmental opportunities; and a host of other factors. Still, there are some commonalities in technical support in the three programs that had formal evaluations: the International Budget Partnership (IBP), the Secretariat for Institutional Support for Economic Research in Africa (SISERA),[11] and the United States Agency for International Development Policy Research Organizations program in Bosnia and Herzegovina (USAID–PRO).[12]

Training has been a component of all three programs, and much of it has been defined by the sponsors, though with some client input. IBP has a standard training program for new partners and provides regular training opportunities with expanded offerings each year. USAID–PRO required training in policy analysis as a condition for grant eligibility. SISERA offered several standard training courses, workshops, and regular supervision visits by its staff.

Two of these three programs (IBP and USAID–PRO) have used the research grant application review process as an opportunity for active mentoring to improve applications, particularly the analytic and communications elements. Both also have provided advice through mentors during the analysis cycle. On-site diagnostics by mentors has been an element of all three programs to define training and mentoring activities with partners. None of the diagnostics has been conducted at baseline, however, which people close to the SISERA and USAID–PRO projects viewed as a limitation. Valuable time was lost in identifying needs.

In addition, the first five programs described in box 6.3 have tried to ensure that the analytic results were effectively fed into the policy development process. The most common requirement has been for applications to include dissemination plans, but some programs have gone further. IBP stresses uptake of results in its analytic trainings. Revenue Watch Institute uses its annual reviews of grantees as an opportunity to assess effectiveness and to work for improvement where needed. The USAID–PRO project used its research grant application process to push for policy relevance.

The TAP and the Strengthening Institutions project models provide limited direct technical assistance, although they do offer resources to help grantees complete their projects. The two models present learning by doing opportunities for supporting recipient organizations in performing analytic work, with an engagement plan for using the results. Each organization applies the same analytic techniques, although in different countries and on different topics. The underlying principles are that people and institutions learn best by doing original, locally determined work using monitoring tools that can be applied to many kinds of problems; that analysis should be explicitly connected to advocacy or constructive engagement with the government so that it does not simply end up on a shelf upon completion; that similar cross-country work will allow organizations to start to benchmark domestic results against those in other countries; that peer review and competition within each cohort will improve the quality of products; that sharing experience in policy engagement across countries will spark more effective practices; and that participating in an international project will bring added visibility and credibility to the organization at home. Clearly this is more of a learning agenda than the institutional development plus technical assistance agenda of the other approaches. It complements these other approaches, taking for granted that they are already providing core support.

Lessons for donors

While rigorous evaluations of donor programs would more clearly reveal the determinants of success in capacity-building efforts, this review of past and current programs, together with information gathered from independent monitoring organizations, offers some broad lessons for improving outside support for independent monitoring organizations.

Focusing on analytic and communication skills and organization management

Experience demonstrates the importance of strengthening the whole organization rather than individual components. The cases highlighted in chapter 5 show that successful organizations need to be analytically competent, adept at evidence-based advocacy and communications, and well managed.

TAP deconstructed *Managing Think Tanks*[13] to develop a questionnaire that systematically assesses the institutional and analytic capacity of an organization in all important dimensions. Parts of this questionnaire supplied the baseline data cited earlier in this chapter. The questionnaire creates a checklist against which any policy organization can benchmark itself (or an outside reviewer could do it). Improving the score is simply a matter of making changes within the institution to reach a higher standard of performance. An investment and management plan can be prepared to accomplish the improvement, and donors can help fund it. Progress can be measured against the standards in the questionnaire. This task is not child's play by any means, but the questionnaire opens up the organizational box to reveal how it functions and where the weaknesses lie.

Building independent monitoring organizations' sense of ownership

Designing a successful capacity-building program requires building a sense of ownership within the organization, which must take responsibility for its own success and for making the most of the support provided. While this lesson may seem obvious, it has for the most part been ignored. On the other hand, some interventions have been so respectful of the autonomy of local organizations that they have not imposed adequate structure on the capacity-building aspects of the relationship and have consequently missed opportunities. How can capacity-building programs make sure that participating institutions have a strong voice in the operation of the program, have something important at risk in the outcome, and yet gain skills they may not have realized they lack? It is common in high-income countries for companies and governments to hire consultants to fill gaps in their capabilities, to advise on institutional strengthening, and to improve managerial performance. This help is fully owned by the organization, which is completely at risk for its success or failure. How can outside technical assistance mimic this situation—or at least come close?

Independent monitoring organizations should have some say in what support they receive. While there are clear efficiencies in having a standard training package, a program without input from the organization is unlikely to be successful. All too often donors would like to direct what the organization does with the donor's money. Mutually agreed goals and benchmarks, a powerful tool for engendering responsibility, are not much in evidence among older programs, but are planned for the Think Tank Initiative.

Selecting independent monitoring organizations for capacity building

A balance must be struck when selecting independent monitoring organizations for capacity-building programs. It is useful to seek organizations with some basic level of capacity to avoid providing assistance to organizations with nothing in place to sustain them. But there is also a tendency to want to identify organizations that have not already been "discovered" by donors and are not already receiving funding from numerous international sources. While donors must decide what balance they want to strike, a common characteristic of successful independent monitoring organizations is a clear expression of interest in institution strengthening and in new substantive projects that may stretch their capabilities.

A fundamental question is how to balance assured long-term funding with accountability. In the survey of independent monitoring organizations discussed earlier in the chapter, there was near unanimity on this point: establish mutually agreed benchmarks at the program's start for first-year outputs and long-term outcomes. These should be supplemented with annual reviews of progress and adjustments in the next year's goals in light of the defined long-term outcome targets. This approach requires a careful baseline diagnosis before the initial discussion.

What if an organization fails? The founder and inspirational leader may depart, personality or ideological clashes may overwhelm the organization, or it may lose its focus and confidence as key staff or funding sources come and go. Little has been written about what donors should do about partner organizations that fail to meet program standards. Good practice would call for some sanctions while the donor works with the organization to identify the underlying causes of failure and to correct them over some reasonable timeframe. Partners that effectively address the problems would be returned to full program participant status.

Strengthening collaboration among independent monitoring organizations— peer learning

While external experts can support independent monitoring organizations in areas of weakness, some of the greatest learning has occurred through the transfer of knowledge among organizations. Peer learning is especially valuable in groups with similar missions but different strengths. In models such as TAP, with a mix of organizations with varied skill levels, organizations have drawn on each other's strengths during peer learning events. Often strong analytical organizations lack the agility and communications capabilities of advocacy groups, which in turn tend to lack analytical skills. Putting them together creates a rich learning environment that can result in enduring professional relationships that are kept intact through the Internet and the telephone.

In addition to peer learning events, donors are increasingly using new technology to connect organizations in different countries and regions during capacity-building programs. While online communities of knowledge are still new in capacity-building programs, this is a potentially cost-effective alternative for donors to explore. Global Development Network, for example, uses a shared online workspace to support its program, giving it a 24 hour presence for its scattered partners.

Strengthening collaboration with decisionmakers and media

The historical image of civil society organizations has been one of opposition to government, with no interest in collaborating on positive change. However, this is changing, and organizations are seeking collaboration with policymakers and other stakeholders as a more effective means of changing the way governments do business. While donors may not have obvious ways to connect independent monitoring organizations with policymakers and media, leaders of capacity-building programs can design assistance to encourage constructive engagement rather than adversarial confrontation.

Capacity-building programs can be designed to convey the importance of engaging decisionmakers, the media, and other stakeholders through a variety of events that build greater acceptance of analytic results and advice. In addition, donors can include legislators and government officials in training events to raise capacity, increase understanding of the work of independent monitoring organizations, and build relationships.

Examples of successful collaborations with media and government include the work of the Center for Democratic Development in Ghana and Guatemala's National Economic Research Center, described in chapter 5. Some of the programs explored in this chapter are applying new methods for formal collaboration between independent monitoring organizations and key audiences, and such approaches are likely to continue to expand.

Understanding the logistics of capacity building—how much and for how long?

In addition to attention to the content and programmatic features of capacity-building assistance, donors need to answer two key questions about the structure of such programs. How much money should be provided, and for how many years?

A challenge is to provide sufficient support to give partner organizations the fiscal space to undertake new and demanding projects and improve their operations without creating dependency or jeopardizing an organization's ability to deliver on its expanded commitments.

In the survey of 14 independent monitoring organizations that participated in the TAP pilot, respondents were asked how much funding their organizations could absorb without creating significant growth-associated problems. The consistent response was 20–30 percent. Two respondents indicated much higher values primarily because of the scalability of their operations: one had a set of regional offices whose activities could be expanded with additional funds, and the other suggested that budget-related fieldwork could be expanded by recruiting and training new mid-level staff. On balance, however, the 20–30 percent range appears reasonable. Such modest amounts of money can strain the ability of donors to think small enough.

As to how long financial support should be provided to permit organizations to achieve desired impacts in policy and institutional development, the general view among independent monitoring organizations interviewed was that individual areas could be strengthened in a year but that overall improvement would take several years because everything cannot be changed at once. As the data suggest, when outside support is a large share of an organization's budget, funds should probably be withdrawn in small increments over a long and predictable period of time. If the resources are withdrawn more suddenly and not replaced, the institution building that the additional resources were to make possible could dissipate.

Respondents made an important clarification in discussing policy impacts. Many organizations thought that they could do the analysis, convince key policymakers of the need for change, and get the necessary legal or regulatory changes within 12–18 months. But if their involvement stopped there, the likelihood that the new policy would actually be implemented was modest at best. Bureaucrats are viewed as resistant to change and unfamiliar with new approaches. Continuing, active support is often essential to maintain the momentum for change. Therefore, activities need to be considered as a cycle of technical assistance in policy analysis and program implementation over three or four years. This implies a minimum total support period of 3–5 years.

While this chapter has looked at a sample of core funding programs, there is also a role for providing short-term project funding for capacity building. The TAP model of support uses project funding to build capacity through learning by doing, enabling independent monitoring organizations to build capacity in analytic and advocacy work related to a specific methodology. It also allows successful organizations to receive continuing funding to expand their projects, providing a complement to traditional multiyear funding.

Building in evaluation from the start

The final lesson for designing and implementing a capacity-building program is related to evaluation. As highlighted in this chapter, many capacity-building programs have been implemented, but few have provided information on the effectiveness and cost-effectiveness of different models. By structuring a credible and comprehensive evaluation program from the outset, recipients and donors alike can learn more about how well their financial and technical support contributes to achieving their program goals. Many leaders of capacity-building programs are starting to think more about the importance of evaluation, and as the results of new evaluations emerge in the next few years, they should provide valuable evidence on effectiveness.[14]

Summary of lessons for improving the effectiveness of independent monitoring organizations

The analysis in this chapter is handicapped by the paucity of rigorous program evaluations. Nevertheless, several lessons have emerged as hypotheses for improving the impact of outside support for independent monitoring organizations:

- Providing longer term funding for core support against a business or research plan is likely to have greater impact on an institution than is shorter term, episodic funding based on specific projects, especially if the topics are donor driven. However, once stable core funding is in place, competitive learning by doing programs can provide complementary support that builds expenditure monitoring skills and exposes organizations to international competition and performance standards.

- Core support that targets management practices, analytic capabilities, and engagement or communication and advocacy skills can benefit from applying readily available knowledge of the operational characteristics of well run think tanks and policy analysis organizations. Benchmarking against this knowledge base or against the practices of other organizations can help an organization measure its development.

- Programs that finance an outsider's idea of what an independent monitoring organization should look like and study are likely to have much less impact on the organization than programs the organization has a core role in designing. This may seem so obvious as to be trite, but donors are often looking for a particular result and see the organizations they are building as a means to that end.

- Organizations that self-select into an institutional-strengthening program should do so because they want to improve institutional capabilities, expenditure monitoring skills, analytical work, and the ability to influence government decisions, not only because they seek additional funding for expansion. For donors, successfully identifying such organizations is another challenge.

- Independent monitoring organizations can learn a lot from each other. However, long experience indicates that simply creating a network—with informal contacts, newsletters, conferences, and training opportunities—does not fully exploit this opportunity nor is it likely to be sustained by the members if outside funds are withdrawn. Structured, intense opportunities to work across borders professionally are another option that shows promise—such experiences develop relationships through content and feedback rather than through informal communications and meetings.

- Outside donor organizations often have contacts with government officials that domestic organizations lack. Outside organizations also bring their own staff or consultants into a country for analytical work. A challenge, well beyond funding for institutional support, is helping to develop independent monitoring organizations by involving them in the regular work of the supportive donor.

- Providing a large share of an organization's budget brings with it the responsibility of long-term support with an incremental exit strategy spelled out at the beginning of the engagement, reviewed regularly, and pursued over a long time.

- An emphasis on being able to conduct credible and timely program evaluations must be built into the program from the outset. The standard method of hiring outside consultants during the last year of a program to conduct a qualitative evaluation does nothing to improve the program as it unfolds, requires that no metrics for success be set out at the start on the basis of a baseline analysis, and is fundamentally incompatible with a program designed to strengthen quantitative and analytic skills.

This guidance is subjective and draws on what little we know from past and current efforts to strengthen independent monitoring organizations. Much more information is needed about the cost effectiveness of different approaches and their sustainability. The cheapest approach may not be the most cost effective, and a combination of approaches—long-term core support, matching grant challenges, short-term competitive grants, technical assistance options—are likely to be more effective than a single option. Evaluation requires numbers and measurement, and efforts to support independent monitoring organizations will not improve until we know more. One thing is certain. It is very difficult for independent monitoring organizations to develop and thrive supported solely by a domestic resource base. Accepting funds from government reduces their independence, and untied domestic sources of charitable finance are extremely scarce. There is definitely an important role for outside funders to jumpstart this capability. Doing it well is the challenge.

Notes

1. On citizen report cards, see Paul (2002) and The Public Affairs Center, an organization Paul founded in Bangalore, India (pacindia.org). Many reviews of this group's pioneering work on citizen report cards are available.

2. See Blagescu and Young (2006), who provide a comprehensive inventory of recent donor initiatives.

3. Struyk (2008) and Struyk, Damon, and Haddaway (2009) are the primary sources of information for this chapter.

4. For a description of these independent monitoring organizations and the work completed under the small grants program, see Kosack, Tolmie, and Griffin (2009).

5. Struyk, Damon, and Haddaway (2009, p. 18). The questionnaire is based on the principles in Struyk (2006). The quality assurance ratings could be done for 18 of the 20 organizations.

6. The full set of countries is Bangladesh, Cameroon, Ghana, India, Indonesia, Kenya, Malawi, Nigeria, Pakistan, Uganda, and Zambia.

7. For further analysis, see Court and others (2006).

8. For detailed explanation and evaluation of programs, see Struyk (2008).

9. See www.acbf-pact.org.

10. IDRC and Hewlett Foundation 2007.

11. Bannock Consulting 2004.

12. Struyk, Kohagen, and Miller 2007.

13. Struyk 2006.

14. Both TAP and the Strengthening Institutions to Improve Public Expenditure Accountability program (led by the Global Development Network) are among programs that have included evaluations in their program design.

Chapter 7

Conclusion—bringing everyone to the same page

This final chapter looks at what all the key players—donors, governments, independent monitoring organizations—can do to strengthen independent monitoring organizations and increase their impact. But first a little background and some additional insight into the story presented in the preface.

The story of the book

The preface tells a story about this book. It shows what the numbers in chapter 2 look like on the ground and describes a dream of how civil society and independent monitoring organizations might improve the situation. This section reflects on what we have learned about that story in the intervening pages of this book.[1]

For the World Bank, the legislator, and the civil society organizations in the preface story, information was everything. The World Bank had access to the budget numbers, invested in getting them organized, and thus understood the problems in a technical way. The legislator knew that information by itself was not enough. Also needed were accessible numbers, a clear storyline, ability to interrogate the data providers and budget preparers, and enough time to consider and act intelligently on the budget—none of it immediately available. The civil society organizations had an abundance of information about what was happening at the end of the chain—in the schools. What they needed was to better understand the context, so that they could take action.

A core theme of this book is that a necessary condition for accountability is that all actors have access to understandable budgets and the resulting resource flows. That is not sufficient, but without accurate, understandable data on spending and its impacts, accountability is virtually impossible. It is the government's responsibility to provide this—at a bare minimum to publish a citizens budget—and not to make the budget so obscure that only professionals at the International Monetary Fund or the World Bank can figure it out.

The budget process has three major elements: prioritization (or allocating resources), execution (or implementation), and evaluation of the result (see figure 4.1 in chapter 4). All three elements are important, and they interact with each other. For the minister of finance in the story, improving execution in the ministry of education opened up the possibility of making resource allocation decisions to improve primary education that had not been feasible before. The ministry of finance began to disburse funds directly to schools to implement the changes—with accountability now residing in the schools rather than in the ministry of education.

As civil society organizations discovered that they could have an impact on resource allocation, they realized that how budgets were implemented was key to getting the desired result. Moving money directly to schools opened up new possibilities for further improvement because civil society organizations and parents could directly pressure headmasters to do a better job.

All of these changes together helped to deal with the resource use problem that blocked everything else. Once that was addressed, it became feasible to think about education quality and opportunities for children to get to secondary school, issues that would benefit from having many minds engaged—preferably some of them with a direct interest in the results for their children—rather than just a few professionals in a ministry of education.

In this story, when the policy discussion was only between the World Bank and the government, the analysis could be perfect but the outcome negligible. Closed-door discussions conducted in English once every 5 or 10 years based on technical documents, coupled with inherently limited and low-power instruments like persuasion and loans, are far less compelling than are debates in the local language, pressed by organizations capable of keeping the focus and pressure on decisionmakers.

The open question is whether there are synergies that could be exploited to improve the impact of all three sets of capabilities and interests—those of governments, independent monitoring organizations, and international agencies. Certainly, in this story, the minister of finance was sympathetic to the World Bank's analysis but could not find a practical way to implement it. And while finding the adversarial nature of the interaction with civil society organizations unwelcome, the minister could not complain about the result. What would need to happen so that all three players would derive benefits from partnering, even while realizing that their interests will not always align perfectly? The World Bank has analyzed the long and short routes of accountability. This book has focused primarily on how to perforate the long route so that citizens can effectively engage with government to improve outcomes.

How can some civil society organizations develop beyond issue-focused advocacy to become partners in the budget process, making the metamorphosis to independent monitoring organizations with both an analytical and advocacy capacity to engage for the long term in all stages of the expenditure cycle?

If everything transpires as in this story, would donors really step up and put additional funding through government systems that work? Would we then witness more coordination and better behavior among donors, lower transactions costs for aid, and higher impact?

Legislatures are missing in action as far as the budget process is concerned in many countries. Independent monitoring organizations are not a substitute for effective legislative oversight. They can make legislatures more effective, but in country after country the legislative oversight agenda is far from complete.

The choice is not between supply-side interventions and demand-side interventions. They are complementary. On the supply side, improving government processes and institutions is essential, but like all investments, it has diminishing marginal impact. Improved government systems may also result from demand-side interventions, as they did in this story.

What has been missing has been a focus on cultivating civil society monitoring institutions as a complement to these investments. However, it is not obvious that governments or international agencies have a particular advantage in helping civil society organizations develop. Independent monitoring organizations almost certainly need help from the outside, both financially and technically, but that help is probably best provided through other civil society organizations rather than directly from governments or international financial institutions.

What can donors do?

Traditional donors are pouring money into efforts to generate domestic demand for good governance. As with all initial efforts in development, the approach is direct: find civil society organizations and give them money, training, networks, and anything else clever, well meaning people can think of that might help.

Perhaps the most important thing traditional donors and international financial institutions can do is something considerably more indirect: address the necessary condition of transparency in the public sector. No matter how well developed or financed, independent monitoring organizations will have limited success if budgets are not public, understandable, and connected to meaningful programs and outcomes or if only part of the budget process works and is open. Transparency can be accomplished at the international level, where donors and international organizations have an absolute advantage. The priority of traditional donors in the governance arena should be to make sure that this necessary condition is in place. The traditional method for doing so is through International Development Association replenishment negotiations and International Monetary Fund and World Bank requirements for borrowing countries. But examples of voluntary pacts abound as well (such as the Extractive Industries Transparency Initiative).

A second priority is the abysmal performance record of governments on the Open Budget Index and Public Expenditure and Financial Accountability standards for legislative review, budget implementation, and auditing/evaluation feedback. Investing to improve these steps in the chain and making sure they also are public, transparent, and accessible will require intense effort over quite a long time.

A surprise in the examination of the World Bank's public expenditure reviews was that each one seemed to be custom designed, with little or no comparability across countries. One would want to see more consistency, with comparable analysis and numbers across countries and perhaps with customizations to account for specific country issues.

Domestic players need less custom design and more international benchmarks. Otherwise, it is impossible to understand how well governments are doing or what their potential performance is—in efficiency and equity of spending but also in service delivery. For the most part, these benchmarks do not exist. This is another area where international players can help. Benchmarks would be extremely helpful for independent monitoring organizations, which could contribute to them if a framework were developed.

Of course money is important for the development of independent monitoring organizations, and donors have it. Chapter 6 suggested that money from the outside is probably essential, that long-term commitments are needed (but with an up-front exit strategy), that the money should probably come through other civil society organizations rather than from governments or international agencies, and that the process needs to be structured in a way that can be evaluated and improved. The amount of funding meeting these criteria today might partially support 100–150 institutions, at the most. The Think Tank Initiative received more than 300 applications (from Africa alone) for fewer than 20 grants.

There is scope to do much more, but small amounts of donor money traveling through many small channels probably cannot create the scale needed to keep track of what is being done, to learn how to improve it, or to have the means to improve it. Some carefully considered institutional work is needed to build up these flows within a strict business-like structure.

Donors need to change the way they do business. Independent monitoring organizations are rarely aware of donor-led analytic work and are rarely asked to participate. Where there is collaboration, it is likely to be through small consulting contracts for specific pieces of work. Discussing donor work programs with civil society organizations and coordinating analytic efforts could create synergies that would stretch the budgets and influence of both parties. Opening up supervision of donor-financed projects to local organizations would fundamentally alter accountability for both the donor and the government.

What can independent monitoring organizations do?

For organizations traditionally operating on a shoestring, kept in the dark (to the extent possible) by governments, and lacking the ability to attract and keep skilled professionals, the opportunities that have arisen in the past few years are a boon. Independent monitoring organizations are fiercely independent and are always looking for branding opportunities that will get their names in front of policymakers. Yet from a development perspective, there is also a role for collective action, both within and across countries. Why shouldn't some of the older and more successful organizations pool resources to develop an international peer-reviewed policy journal, produce benchmarks for members as a method of raising quality and institutional standards, develop new technologies for monitoring governments in their own environments, and take ownership of the training and small grants programs now being conducted on their behalf by outside institutions?

One of the greatest dangers of the increased donor funding is the development of rogue "NGIs"—an affectionate term for nongovernment individuals—who can convince donors of the value of funding them. An effort to develop professional standards can only benefit this infant industry as a whole.

What can governments do?

Without hesitation, ministries of finance need to review systems of accountability and explore options to make sector ministries more accountable to their clients. The ministry of finance's fiduciary and control functions are more in line with the interests of independent monitoring organizations than with those of sector ministries. Often, ministries of finance feel that they are dropping blank checks into the black holes of education and health spending; improving the accountability of those ministries to citizens can only help to ease this concern. While keeping accountability agents at arm's length, ministries of finance should certainly be able to find ways to support independent monitoring organizations indirectly to achieve greater openness and accountability of sector ministries.

Legislatures must become more engaged in the budget process and in accounting for results at year end. They require considerable reform and support so that they can weigh in intelligently and effectively on expenditures.

Why should low- and middle-income countries wait for donor countries to organize to require greater transparency, better budget processes, and citizen-friendly governments? Performance by low- and middle-income countries on the Open Budget Index ranges widely, and there is no reason why some of the good performers could not lead a self-improvement campaign. Transparency not only makes for good government but can also translate into capital inflows, growth, and opportunities for citizens to prosper. Chile, for example, has shown how consistent improvements in the robustness of public financial management and procurement processes can make a country more attractive to international investors. For the new member states in the European Union, adopting higher standards of public budgeting, procurement, and accountability coincided with large inflows of public and private funds.

And finally, a ministry of finance perspective

We close with an extended quotation from Goodall Edward Gondwe, Minister of Finance of Malawi in 2004–09, from a seminar at the Brookings Institution on October 18, 2007:[2]

> Let me start by saying that the involvement of civil society in the budgetary process or, indeed, in economic policy formulation, is new. In the British system that I think Nigeria, Malawi, and other English-speaking countries follow—and I'm sure my colleague for Burkina Faso is here, this is true of the French system also—it used to be that the budget was a secret document. People prepared it secretly, and then it went to Parliament. And even Parliament was shown the estimates, expenditure estimates, but never quite what you wanted to say as far as taxes were concerned. Only the last day did you open up and let the world know what you wanted to do.
>
> This . . . was supposed to be the case. Formulation of policies and plans were done by the government, discussed with Parliament very much

within the confines of the constitutional bodies. You were very much surprised if civil society outside the constitutional institutions got involved in the process.

So I'd like to say that this, what we're discussing here, involvement of civil society, is new. And I think a lot of the problems that we've had with civil society in this process is because of that. Both the civil society is trying to see what to do, and what to do with opportunities now available to them, to get involved. And the government people also do not quite know just what to do with these people who are upstarts in the job. Let me describe what is happening in Malawi.

. . . As far as Malawi is concerned, one can divide civil society organizations involved in the budget or, should I say, economic activities of the government, into two. One group is very much concerned with the revenue aspects of the budget. You have the accountant society. You have the chamber of commerce. You have institutions like the University Economic Society and institutions of that sort. They are also civil society organizations. They are not as obnoxious as the others, but nevertheless they are.

Our experience is that we have derived a lot of advantage from getting the accountants involved in the budget field. Every year, almost religiously, some four or five months before the budget itself, we have a series of meetings with these people who will advise and come out very strongly as to how they see the fiscal system running, in particular what sort of taxes, what's wrong with this tax, and what could be improved. And I find that in most cases very good points of view are taken, technically very sound.

In Malawi, like a number of African countries, we are now involved in trying to clean up the economies, to get them attractive to the private sector, to get them to be more competitive. And the tax system is an aspect that we're trying to improve in that sense. And we have gained a lot from civil society, these meetings that I'm talking about. There are some outrageous proposals that we get. We discard those. But by and large, we have had some advantage in involving the civil society in those aspects of the budget.

On the other side is the expenditure side, of course. . . . There are two things involved as far as economic policy is concerned. We have [what] a number of people call the "PRSP" [Poverty Reduction Strategy] document, where we find that civil society has been very, very active in putting it forward. . . . Sometimes I wondered whether we were talking to Malawians. In most cases we were talking to, I think, NGOs [nongovernmental organizations] from outside Africa who had infiltrated the ranks of the Malawians.

And the point of view that they expressed in some cases was not all that Malawian. I will give you an example. The Malawians typically think that in the medium term or the long term we really should be concerned with growth of the economy and that poverty reduction will follow. When you look at the PRSP and what the NGOs officially were concerned with, they were religiously pursuing what one would call "the Washington consensus" that strongly feels that the main objective would be poverty reduction. The two should not be all that different. But the point is that there are some policies that you can pursue that will have poverty reduction in front and growth behind. I found that there was a problem there. Let me not go too much into that.

On the budget itself, we felt—I still feel—. . . I got the impression that my staff were rather reluctant to be so liberal in putting forward information to these upstarts. Why? Sometimes I sympathized, because there is a complete misuse of the information. First, very few, unless they are penetrated farther by the western NGOs, quite understand what these figures really are about and what they imply. And so when they go to the press to tell the public what is happening, most of the interpretation of what is happening is really, really very wrong and, in some cases, quite dangerous in a way. And so you are, if you are in government, you are rather worried that these upstarts, they're up to no good, they just want to damage the reputation of the government. And therefore why give them the information?

On the other hand, I have found it very, very interesting that there are some who do a very good, thorough job dividing themselves into sectors. They are able to take on the government on various sectors like education, and they will go into the depth of whether the expenditure on primary education or university education or secondary education is really, really optimal. And they can go into the depth of a discussion of that. I find that sometimes it may not be important that year, but the next year I am able to look at what they said and see whether we can make use of it. So there are advantages sometimes.

The second thing is that they are—because in some cases they are specialized—they are able to come out with information that is beneficial to members of Parliament, to tell them really the intricacies of what the budget means for the sectors in which they're interested—in agriculture, in health, in education, and what have you.

So where they are specialized, where you've got good people there, they can be very helpful. But the trouble is that most of them play to the galleries. And that's where probably . . . there is need, if they are to be helpful, for us or the NGOs in the West to invest in their education so that they actually understand and are able to even articulate what they want to say, and to understand what those figures mean.

Let me end by saying that there used to be a time when we thought that these [civil society organizations] were upstarts, they will go away at some stage. So, tolerate them for some time. They'll go away.

Well, it doesn't seem so. They will not go. And therefore I think it's important that we should reach a point where we should concentrate on how you can make them to be even more helpful to the government as well as to society as a whole. They are part, now, of the process, the budgetary process. You have to accept it. But I think . . . some of them will have to be going in for a further education and stop playing to the galleries. That's not their job.

Secondly, in Malawi there is a weakness—. . . in Malawi they're not interested so much about how projects are being implemented. They are not. They have not got involved in procurement issues. They are not interested in these things because I don't think they think that they're sexy enough. But I hope very much that they can get involved in that, too. As far as Malawi is concerned—I don't see any Malawians here so I can say it—there is need for that.

When a fine and insightful speaker from the trenches eloquently summarizes this book, that is a fit ending.

Notes

1. Readers might want to go back and have a look at the preface at this point.
2. The Brookings Institution 2007.

References

Ablo, Emmanuel, and Ritva Reinikka. 1998. "Do Budgets Really Matter? Evidence from Public Spending on Education and Health in Uganda." Policy Research Working Paper 1926. World Bank, Washington, DC.

Ahmad, Junaid, Shanta Devarajan, Stuti Khemani, and Shekhar Shah. 2005. "Decentralization and Service Delivery." Policy Research Working Paper 3603. World Bank, Washington, DC.

Alvarado, Betty, and Eduardo Morón. 2007. "Towards a Results-Based Budget." Research Center of the University of the Pacific (CIUP), Lima. Available at http://tap.resultsfordevelopment.org/resources/towards-results-based-budget.

Andrews, Matthew, and Anwar Shah. 2003. "Towards Citizen-oriented Local-level Budgets in Developing Countries." In *Ensuring Accountability When There is No Bottom Line*, ed. Anwar Shah. Washington, DC: World Bank.

Ascher, William. 1998. "From Oil to Timber: The Political Economy of Off-Budget Development Financing in Indonesia." *Indonesia* 65 (April): 37–61.

Bannock Consulting. 2004. "Evaluation of the Secretariat for Institutional Support for Economic Research in Africa." IDRC Report. International Development Research Centre, Ottawa.

Bellver, A., and Kaufmann, D. 2005. "Transparenting Transparency: Initial Empirics and Policy Implications." Policy Research Working Paper. World Bank, Washington, DC.

Besley, Timothy, and Robin Burgess. 2002. "The Political Economy of Government Responsiveness: Theory and Evidence from India." *Quarterly Journal of Economics* 117 (4) 1415–51.

Besley, Timothy, Rohini Pande, Lupin Rahman, and Vijayendra Rao. 2004. "The Politics of Public Good Provision: Evidence from Indian Local Governments." *Journal of the European Economic Association* 2 (2–3): 416–26.

BIGS (Bandung Institute of Governance Studies). 2008. "Local Innovations on Public Spending Management in Indonesia." BIGS, West Java, Indonesia. Available at http://tap.resultsfordevelopment.org/resources/local-innovations-public-spending-management-indonesia.

Blagescu, M., and J. Young. 2006. "Capacity Building for Policy Advocacy: Current Thinking and Approaches among Agencies Supporting Civil Society Organizations." Working Paper 260. Overseas Development Institute, London.

Brizuela Speratti, Cynthia. 2008 "Education Expenditures: Budget Tracking Analysis of Thirty Paraguayan Educational Institutions." Working Paper. Centro de Analisis y Difusion de la Economia Paraguaya, Asunción.

The Brookings Institution. 2007. "Ministries of Finance and Civil Society Organizations: Friends or Foes?" October 18, 2007, Washington, DC. Transcript available at http://www.brookings.edu/~/media/Files/events/2007/1018ministries/20071018.pdf.

Brosio, Giorgio. 2000. "Decentralization in Africa." Paper presented at the Conference on Fiscal Decentralization, November 20–21. International Monetary Fund, Fiscal Affairs Department, Washington, DC.

Caddy, Joanne, Tiago Peixoto, and Mary McNeil. 2007. "Beyond Public Scrutiny: Stocktaking of Social Accountability in OECD Countries." WBI Working Paper. World Bank Institute and Organisation for Economic Co-operation and Development, Washington, DC.

CBPS (Center for Budget and Policy Studies). 2007. "Expenditure on Education and Health at the Local Level." Center for Budget and Policy Studies, Bengaluru, India. Available at http://tap.resultsfordevelopment.org/resources/expenditure-health-and-education-two-districts.

CDD (Center for Democratic Development). 2008. "Tracking Leakage of Public Resources in Education: A Pilot Investigation of Teacher Absence in Public Primary Schools in Ghana." Center for Democratic Development, Transparency and Accountability Project, The Brookings Institution, Washington, DC. Available at http://tap.resultsfordevelopment.org/resources/tracking-absentee-rates-among-primary-school-teachers-ghana.

CIPPEC (Center for the Implementation of Public Policies Promoting Equity and Growth). 2008. "Equity and Effectiveness of Public Expenditure in Schools in Argentina." Center for the Implementation of Public Policies Promoting Equity and Growth, Buenos Aires. Available at http://tap.resultsfordevelopment.org/resources/equity-and-effectiveness-expenditure-schools-argentina.

CIVICUS. 2006. "Civil Society Index: Preliminary Findings Phase 2003–2005." CIVICUS, Johannesburg, South Africa.

Corporacion Latinobarometro. 2009. "Informe Latinobarometro 2009." November, Santiago, Chile. Available at www.latinobarometro.org. summarizes the report annually in English. A report summary appears in "The Latinobarómetro Poll: A Slow Maturing of Democracy," *The Economist,* December 10, 2009.

Court, J., E. Mendizabel, D. Osbourne, and J. Young. 2006. *Policy Engagement: How Civil Society Can Be More Effective.* London: Overseas Development Institute.

Cuevas, Mario, and Jorge Lavarreda. 2008. "Expenditure Tracking to Improve the Effectiveness of Public Education in Guatemala." National Centre for Economic Research (CIEN), Guatemala City. Available at http://tap.resultsfordevelopment.org/resources/expenditure-tracking-improve-effectiveness-public-education-guatemala.

Davoodi, H.R., S. Sachjapinan, and J. Kim. 2001. "How Useful Are Benefit Incidence Studies?" World Bank, Washington, DC.

De Ferranti, D., J. Jacinto, A.J. Ody, and G. Ramshaw. 2009. *How to Improve Governance: A Framework for Analysis and Action.* Washington, DC: The Brookings Institution.

De Mello, Luiz. 2004. "Fiscal Decentralization and Subnational Expenditure Policy." International Monetary Fund, Washington DC.

De Renzio, Paolo. 2005. "CSOs and Budgets: Linking Evidence and Pro-Poor Policies." Brief. Overseas Development Institute, London.

———. 2009. "Taking Stock: What Do PEFA Assessments Tell Us about PFM Systems across Countries?" Working Paper 302. Overseas Development Institute, London. Available at www.odi.org.uk/resources/download/3333.pdf.

De Renzio, Paolo, and Warren Krafchik. 2006. "Lessons from the Field: The Impact of Civil Society Budget Analysis and Advocacy in Six Countries. Practitioner's Guide." International Budget Project, Washington, DC.

DFID (U.K. Department for International Development). 2006. *Making Governance Work for the Poor.* White Paper 3. London: U.K. Department for International Development.

Edelman. 2007. "Edelman Trust Barometer 2007." Edelman, New York. Available at www.edelman.com/trust/2007.

Eisenhardt, K. 1989. "Agency Theory: An Assessment and Review." *Academy of Management Review* 14 (1): 57–74.

Farvacque-Vitkovi, C, and L. Godin. 1997. "The Future of African Cities: Challenges and Priorities for Urban Development." World Bank, Washington, DC.

Fioramonti, L., and V.F. Heinrich. 2007. "How Civil Society Influences Policy: A Comparative Analysis of the CIVICUS Civil Society Index in Post-Communist Europe." Research Report. CIVICUS, Johannesburg, South Africa, and Overseas Development Institute, London.

Fleshman, Michael. 2002. "'Gender Budgets' Seek More Equity: Improved Spending Priorities Can Benefit All Africans." *Africa Renewal* 16 (1): 4. Available at www.un.org/ecosocdev/geninfo/afrec/vol16no1/161wm.htm.

Folscher, Alta, and Neil Cole. 2006. "From Policy Agendas to Policies in South Africa." In *Bridging the Gap: From Policies to Budget*, ed. Alta Folscher. Pretoria, South Africa: Collaborative Africa Budget Reform Initiative Secretariat.

Freedom House. 2010. *Freedom in the World 2010: The Annual Survey of Political Rights and Civil Liberties.* Washington, DC: Rowman and Littlefield.

Freire, Mila, and John E. Petersen. 2004. *Subnational Capital Markets in Developing Countries: From Theory to Practice.* New York: Oxford University Press.

Fung, A., M. Graham, and D. Weil. 2007. *Full Disclosure: The Perils and Promise of Transparency.* Cambridge, U.K.: Cambridge University Press.

Global Integrity. 2008. *Global Integrity Report 2007—Key Findings.* Washington, DC: Global Integrity. Available at www.globalintegrity.org/documents/KeyFindings2007.pdf.

IBP/OBI (International Budget Partnership/Open Budget Initiative). 2009. *Open Budgets Transform Lives: The Open Budget Survey 2008.* Washington, DC: International Budget Partnership, Center on Budget and Policy Priorities. Available at http://openbudgetindex. org/.

IDB (Inter-American Development Bank). 2004. "Strategy for Promoting Citizen Participation in Bank Activities." May 19. Inter-American Development Bank, Washington DC.

IDRC (International Development Research Centre) and Hewlett Foundation. 2007. "The Think Tank Initiative: Strengthening Policy Research for Development." International Development Research Centre, Ottawa, and Hewlett Foundation, Palo Alto, Calif.

IDPMS (Indo-Dutch Project Management Society). 2008. "Following the Health Delivery Trail." Indo-Dutch Project Management Society, Bengaluru, India. Available at http://tap.results-fordevelopment.org/resources/following-health-delivery-trail.

IMF (International Monetary Fund). 1999. "Manual on Fiscal Transparency." International Monetary Fund, Department of Fiscal Affairs, Washington, DC.

———. 2001. "Tracking of Poverty-Reducing Public Spending in Heavily Indebted Poor Countries (HIPCs)." March. International Monetary Fund, Washington, DC.

———. 2006. "Standards and Codes: The Role of the IMF." Fact Sheet, March. International Monetary Fund, Washington, DC.

———. Various years. "Reports on the Observance of Standards and Codes (ROSCs)." IMF Reports. International Monetary Fund, Washington, DC.

Institute for Urban Economics. 2007. "Public Health and Education Expenditures Analysis in the Russian Federation in 2004–2006." Working Paper. Institute for Urban Economics, Moscow. Available at http://tap.resultsfordevelopment.org/resources/budget-expenditures-education-and-healthcare-russia-2004-2007.

IPAR (Institute of Policy Analysis and Research). 2008. "Expenditure Tracking of Secondary Education Bursary Scheme in Kenya." Institute of Policy Analysis and Research, Nairobi. Available at http://tap.resultsfordevelopment.org/resources/expenditure-tracking-secondary-education-bursary-scheme-kenya.

Islam, R. 2003. "Do More Transparent Governments Govern Better?" Policy Research Working Paper 3077. World Bank, Washington, DC.

Kaufmann, D., A. Kraay, and M. Mastruzzi. 2007. "Governance Matters VI: Aggregate and Individual Governance Indicators 1996–2006." Policy Research Working Paper 4280. World Bank, Washington, DC.

Khemani, Stuti. 2006. "Local Government Accountability for Health Service Delivery in Nigeria." *Journal of African Economies* 15 (2): 285–312.

Kibua, Thomas, Lineth N. Oyugi, Andrew Riechi, and Evelyn Anupi. 2008. "Expenditure Tracking of Secondary Education Bursary Scheme in Nairobi Province, Kenya." Working Paper. Institute of Policy Analysis and Research, Nairobi. Available at http://tap.resultsfordevelopment.org/resources/expenditure-tracking-secondary-education-bursary-scheme-kenya.

Kosack, S., C. Tolmie, and C. Griffin. 2010. *From the Ground Up: Improving Government Performance with Independent Monitoring Organizations.* Washington, DC: Results for Development Institute and Brookings Institution.

Krafchik, W., and J. Werner. 2004. "Legislatures and Budget Oversight: Best Practices." Paper presented at the Open Forum, April 8, Kazakhstan Revenue Watch, International Budget Project, Almaty. Available at http://archive.revenuewatch.org/reading/051804.shtml.

Ladipo, Omowunmi, Alfonso Sanchez, and Jamil Sopher. 2009. "Effective and Transparent Governance of Public Expenditure in Latin America and the Caribbean: Revitalizing Reforms in Financial Management and Procurement." Working Paper. World Bank, Latin American and Caribbean Region, and Brookings Institution, Transparency and Accountability Project, Washington, DC.

Lane, J.-E. 2005. *Public Administration and Public Management: The Principal-Agent Perspective.* London: Routledge.

Lee, Robert D., Ronald W. Johnson, and Philip G. Joyce. 2007. *Public Budgeting Systems.* Maynard, MA: Jones and Bartlett Publishers.

Lewicki, Roy, and Edward Tomlinson. 2003. "Trust and Trust Building: Beyond Intractability." In *Beyond Intractability,* ed. Guy Burgess and Heidi Burgess. Boulder, CO: University of Colorado, Conflict Research Consortium.

Lipscomb, Andrew, and Albert Bergh, eds. 1907. *The Writings of Thomas Jefferson.* Washington DC: The Thomas Jefferson Memorial Association.

Miller, C. 2007. "Policy Analysis and Dialogue Organizations, Bosnia and Herzegovina—Final Project Report, September 2003–June 2007." Report to USAID–Bosnia. Urban Institute, Washington, DC.

MORI Social Research Institute. 2003. "Trust in Public Institutions—New Findings: National Quantitative Survey." Report for the Audit Commission. MORI, London.

Mountfield, Edward, and Christine P.W. Wong. 2005. "Public Expenditure on the Frontline: Toward Effective Management by Subnational Governments." In *East Asia Decentralizes: Making Local Government Work.* Washington, DC: World Bank.

Mundal, H. 2008. "Public Financial Management Performance Report, Norway—Based on PEFA Methodology." Norwegian Agency for Development Cooperation, Oslo.

Nyman, C., F. Nilsson, and B. Rapp. 2005. "Accountability in Local Government: A Principal-Agent Perspective." *Journal of Human Resource Costing and Accounting* 9 (2): 123–37.

OECD (Organisation for Economic Co-operation and Development). 2001. "OECD Best Practices for Budget Transparency." *OECD Journal of Budgeting* 1 (3) 7–14. Available at www.oecd.org/gov/budget/journal.

———. 2006. *The Challenge of Capacity Development: Working towards Good Practice.* DAC Guidelines and Reference Series. Paris: Organisation for Economic Co-operation and Development.

Okonjo-Iwela, Ngozi and Philip Osafo-Kwaako. 2008. "The Role of Civil Society Organizations in Supporting Fiscal Transparency in African Countries: Some Lessons from Nigeria. Available at www.resultsfordevelopment.org/publications/role-civil-society-organizations-supporting-fiscal-transparency-african-countries.

Paul, Samuel. 2002. *Holding the State to Account: Citizen Monitoring in Action.* Bengaluru, India: Books for Change.

Pearce, David. 1999. "Advancing Subsidy Reform: Towards a Viable Policy Package." Report of the Fifth Expert Group on Finance for Sustainable Development. United Nations Department of Economic and Social Affairs, Nairobi.

PEFA Secretariat. 2005. "Public Financial Management Performance Measurement Framework." World Bank, Washington DC. Available at www.pefa.org/pfm_performance_frameworkmn.php.

Pradhan, Sanjay. 1996. *Evaluating Public Spending: A Framework for Public Expenditure Reviews.* Discussion Paper 323. Washington, DC: World Bank.

Psacharopoulos, George, and Harry A. Patrinos. 2002. "Returns to Investment in Education: A Further Update." Policy Research Working Paper 2881. World Bank, Washington, DC.

Ramkumar, V. 2007a. "Expanding Collaboration between Public Audit Institutions and Civil Society." International Budget Project, Washington, DC.

———. 2007b. "Monitoring Government Budget Expenditures: A Guide for Civil Society Organizations." Draft. International Budget Project, Washington, DC.

———. 2008. *Our Money, Our Responsibility: A Citizen's Guide to Monitoring Government Expenditures.* Washington, DC: International Budget Project.

Ramkumar, V., and W. Krafchik. 2005. "The Role of Civil Society Organizations in Auditing and Public Finance Management." International Budget Project, Washington, DC.

———. 2007. "Can Civil Society Engagement in Budgeting Processes Build Trust in Government?" International Budget Project, Washington, DC.

Ramshaw, G. 2007. "Independent Monitoring Organizations: A Qualitative Look at Performance." The Brookings Institution, Washington, DC.

Rao, Madhusudhan, and Sharadini Rath, ed. 2005. "Study of Municipal Finances in Karnataka." Center for Budget and Policy Studies, Bangalore, India. Available at www.cbps.in.

Reinikka, Ritva, and Jakob Svensson. 2000. "How Inadequate Provision of Public Infrastructure and Services Affects Private Investment." Policy Research Working Paper 2262. World Bank, Washington, DC.

———. 2004. "The Power of Information : Evidence from a Newspaper Campaign to Reduce Capture." Policy Research Working Paper 3239. World Bank, Washington, DC.

Robinson, M. 2006. "Budget Analysis and Policy Advocacy: The Role of Nongovernmental Public Action." Working Paper 279. University of Sussex, Institute of Development Studies, Brighton, U.K.

Rubin, Barnett R., Humayun Hamidzada, and Abby Stoddard. 2003. "Afghanistan Reconstruction Project—Through the Fog of Peacebuilding: Evaluating the Reconstruction of Afghanistan." New York University, Program on Conflict Prevention, Recovery, and Peacebuilding, Center on International Cooperation, New York. Available at www.cic.nyu.edu/.

Sachs, Jeffrey. 2005. "The Development Challenge." *Foreign Affairs* 84 (2): 78–90.

Salamon, L. 2004. "How Healthy Is Your Civil Society Sector?" *Alliance* 9 (2): 12–14.

Shah, Anwar, 2006. "A Practitioner's Guide to Intergovernmental Fiscal Transfers." Policy Research Working Paper 4039. World Bank, Washington, DC.

SIGMA (Support for Improvement in Governance and Management in Central and Eastern European Countries). 2002. "Czech Republic Public Service and the Administrative Framework Assessment." Civil Service Assessment. Organisation for Economic Co-operation and Development and European Union, Paris.

Smith, R, and M. Bertozzi. 1998. "Principals and Agents: An Explanatory Model for Public Budgeting." *Journal of Public Budgeting, Accounting, and Financial Management* 10 (3): 325–52.

Speratti, Cynthia B. 2008. "Education Expenditures: A Budget Tracking Analysis of Thirty Paraguayan Educational Institutions." The Brookings Institution and Results for Development Institute, Washington, DC. Available at http://tap.resultsfordevelopment.org/resources/education-expenditures-budget-tracking-analysis-thirty-paraguayan-educational-institutions.

Stevens, Mike. 2004. "Institutional and Incentive Issues in Public Financial Management Reform in Poor Countries." Public Expenditure and Financial Accountability Program Discussion Paper. World Bank, Washington, DC.

Strömberg, D. 2004. "Radio's Impact on Public Spending," *Quarterly Journal of Economics* 119 (1) 189–221.

Struyk, R. 2006. *Managing Think Tanks*. Budapest and Washington, DC: Open Society Institute Press and Urban Institute Press.

———. 2008. "Options for Supporting Independent Monitoring Organizations." National Opinion Research Center, Washington, DC.

Struyk, R., M. Damon, and S. Haddaway. 2009. "Evaluation of the Transparency and Accountability Project: Baseline Report." National Opinion Research Center, Bethesda, MD.

Struyk, R., K. Kohagen, and C. Miller. 2007. "Were Bosnian Policy Research Organizations More Effective in 2006 than in 2003? Did Technical Assistance Make a Difference?" *Public Administration and Development* 27 (5): 426–38.

Transparency International. 2009. *Global Corruption Report 2009.* Berlin: Transparency International.

Tuck, L., and K. Lindert. 1996. *From Universal Food Subsidies to a Self-Targeted Program: A Case Study in Tunisian Reform.* Discussion Paper 351. Washington, DC: World Bank.

UNCDF (United Nations Capital Development Fund). 2006. *Achieving Results: Performance Budgeting in the Least Developed Countries.* New York: United Nations.

UNDP (United Nations Development Programme). 1990. *Human Development Report 1990.* New York: Oxford University Press.

UNESCO (United Nations Educational, Scientific, and Cultural Organization). 2003. *Scolarisation primaire universelle: un objectif pour tous. Document Statistique.* Paris: Ministers of Education of African States VIII.

———. 2006. *World Education Report.* Paris: United Nations Educational, Scientific, and Cultural Organization.

United Nations. 2007. *The Millennium Development Goals Report 2007.* New York: United Nations.

United Nations General Assembly. 2000. "United Nations Millennium Declaration." United Nations General Assembly Resolution, A/RES/55/2. United Nations General Assembly, New York.

USAID (U.S. Agency for International Development). 2005. *At Freedom's Frontiers: A Democracy and Governance Strategic Framework.* Washington, DC: U.S. Agency for International Development.

Vyasulu, Vinod. 2008. "The Quest for Transparency and Accountability in Governance in India: An Introspection." Center for Budget and Policy Studies, Bangalore, India. Available at www.resultsfordevelopment.org/publications/quest-transparency-and-accountability-governance-india-introspection.

Williamson, O. 1985. *The Economic Institutions of Capitalism.* New York: Free Press.

World Bank. 1993. *World Development Report 1993: Investing in Health.* Washington, DC: World Bank.

———. 1999. "Consumer Food Subsidy Programs in the MENA Region." Report 19561-MNA. World Bank, Human Development Group, Middle East and North Africa Region, Washington, DC.

———. 2001. "Zambia Public Expenditure Review: Public Expenditure, Growth, and Poverty—A Synthesis." Report 22543-ZA. World Bank, Washington, DC.

———. 2002a. "Mongolia Public Expenditure and Financial Management Review: Bridging the Public Expenditure Management Gap ." Report 24439-MOG. World Bank, Washington, DC.

————. 2002b. "National Development and Sub-National Finance in China: A Review of Provincial Expenditures." Report 22951-CHA. World Bank, Washington, DC.

————. 2003a. "Argentina: Reforming Policies and Institutions for Efficiency and Equity of Public Expenditures." Report 25991. World Bank, Washington, DC.

————. 2003b. "Armenia Public Expenditure Review" Report 24370-BD. World Bank, Washington, DC.

————. 2003c. "Bangladesh Public Expenditure Review." Report 24370-BD. World Bank, Washington, DC.

————. 2003d. *World Development Report 2004: Making Services Work for Poor People.* Washington, DC: World Bank and Oxford University Press.

————. 2004a. "Ecuador: Creating Fiscal Space for Poverty Reduction." Report 28911-EC. World Bank, Washington, DC.

————. 2004b. "Ethiopia Public Expenditure Review, Volume I, Public Spending in the Social Sectors 2000–2020: The Emerging Challenge." Report 29338-ET. World Bank, Washington, DC.

————. 2004c. "Pakistan Public Expenditure Management: Strategic Issues and Reform Agenda." Volume I. Report 25665-PK. World Bank, Washington, DC.

————. 2005a. "Chile: Country Financial Accountability Assessment." Report 32630-CL. World Bank, Washington, DC.

————. 2005b. "Kenya Public Expenditure Review 2004: Report on the Structure and Management of Public Spending." Report 29421-KE. World Bank, Washington, DC.

————. 2005c. "Public Financial Management, Procurement, and Expenditure Systems in Iran." Report 34777-IR. World Bank, Washington, DC.

————. 2005d. "Republic of Uzbekistan Public Expenditure Review." Report 31014-UZ. World Bank, Washington, DC.

————. 2005e. "Russia: Fiscal Costs of Structural Reform." Report 30741-RU. World Bank, Washington, DC.

————. 2005f. "United Republic of Tanzania Public Expenditure and Financial Accountability Review—FY05." Report 36642-TZ. World Bank, Washington, DC.

————. 2005g. "Vietnam: Managing Public Expenditure for Poverty Reduction and Growth." Volume 1. Report 30035-Vietnam. World Bank, Washington, DC.

————. 2006a. "Nigeria—Utilization of Repatriated Abacha Loot: Results of the Field Monitoring Exercise." World Bank Working Paper. Washington, DC. All five volumes are available at http://go.worldbank.org/BAHBACH5Q0.

————. 2006b. "Strengthening Bank Group Engagement on Governance and Anticorruption." World Bank, Washington, DC.

————. 2006c. "Swaziland Public Expenditure Review, Volume I, Main Report Strengthening Public Expenditure Policy and Management for Service Delivery and Poverty Reduction." Report 35318-SW. World Bank, Washington, DC.

————. 2007a. "Nigeria: A Fiscal Agenda for Change Public Expenditure Management and Financial Accountability Review (PEMFAR), Volume I: Main Report." Report 35318-SW. World Bank, Washington, DC.

————. 2007b. "Indonesia Public Expenditure Review: Spending for Development: Making the Most of Indonesia's New Opportunities." World Bank, Jakarta.

————. 2007c. *World Development Report 2008: Agriculture for Development.* Washington, DC: World Bank.

————. 2009a. "The World Bank Group Program of Support for the Chad-Cameroon Petroleum Development and Pipeline Construction Program Performance Assessment Report." Report 50315. Independent Evaluation Group, World Bank, Washington, DC.

————.2009b. *World Development Indicators 2009.* Washington, DC: World Bank.

Index